RISING
TO
THE TOP

INSIGHT PUBLISHING
SEVIERVILLE, TENNESSEE

RISING TO THE TOP

© 2007 by Insight Publishing Company.

Disclaimer: This book is a compilation of ideas from numerous experts who have each contributed a chapter. As such, the views expressed in each chapter are of those who were interviewed and not necessarily of the interviewer or Insight Publishing.

Published by Insight Publishing Company
P.O. Box 4189
Sevierville, Tennessee 37864

10 9 8 7 6 5 4 3 2

Printed in the United States of America

ISBN-13: 978-1-60013-160-8
ISBN-10: 1-60013-160-3

Table of Contents

A Message from the Publisher

The finest and best rise to the top. Like cream in milk, people who excel in what they do rise head and shoulders above others in a crowd. How do they do it? Are they born with some driving force that pushes them along? Do they just suddenly decide they're going to do what it takes to rise above or do they just suddenly find themselves there?

I really wanted to find the answers to those questions so I looked for some outstanding people who would tell me what rising to the top means to them and how they rose to the top. I believe I found some folks who gave me some remarkable insights into how they did it. What they told me altered my perception of what rising to the top means—how it's done, why it's done, and most interesting of all, who is able to do it.

You will really be fascinated with what these authors have to say and I think the concepts they present will stretch your mind and give you a unique learning experience. You will have the facts you need to make important decisions about your rise to the top. Yes, it's possible for you to get there and sometimes it just takes that extra boost, that extra bit of knowledge to fill in the gaps. This book is not for those who are satisfied with mediocrity. It is for those of you who really want to know how you can "rise to the top."

Interviews conducted by:
David E. Wright
President, International Speakers Network

Chapter 1

Victoria Rayner

THE INTERVIEW

David Wright (Wright)

Today we're talking with Victoria L. Rayner. Victoria is an author, health care and financial educator, and clinical associate pioneer of a medical sub-specialty involving esthetic care for disfigured and terminally ill patients. She is a columnist and writes about career building and business development. Victoria is also a professional speaker and the subject of biographical record in the Marquis *Who's Who of American Women/Medicine and Health Care.* She is a Member of the American Medical Woman's Association, Honorary Chairman of the Business Advisory Council in Washington, D.C., and Research Scholar at the Library of Congress. Victoria is cited as one of the top business leaders in the country by *The Wall Street Journal* that is using her diverse professional knowledge in the fields of both medicine and business along with her get-it-done attitude to assist nurses and physicians to learn business practices and principles to better deal with the critical economic issues affecting the highly-compromised world of health and patient care today.

Victoria, you are a woman who has become successful in two highly diverse professional worlds—medicine and business. How did that come about?

Victoria Rayner (Rayner)

A certain amount of my business capability was imposed on me by my mother who raised my brother and me as a single parent. She was my role model. I grew up working in her businesses and I was responsible from a very early age to contribute financially to our household expenses.

The world of medicine for me was a passion and gaining entry into it one of the greatest challenges I have ever known. I have always tried to do what people have told me could not be done.

Wright

With success come some amazing rewards—money, power, recognition, influence, and prestige. What do you believe has been the greatest payoff to date?

Rayner

Personal fulfillment.

Wright

You have traveled a rather unconventional career path; is there a reason you chose such an uncharted course for yourself?

Rayner

The development of my career as a clinical faculty associate at a university-hospital and director of my own clinic in the dermatology department was initially the result of pure circumstance. At the age of eighteen I sustained a facial burn injury that left me disfigured for several years.

My experience gave me first-hand knowledge of what it was like to be scarred in public and to be forced to answer unwanted and invasive questions about my flawed appearance. I was living on my own at the time and desperately needed to support myself so I was forced, through a series of trial-and-error episodes, to devise a cosmetic method to conceal my scarring in public. The camouflage method was successful enough that I was able to deceive the interviewers of a major airline who hired me as a stewardess, never knowing I was mutilated under the cosmetic disguise I created.

I flew for several years and during this period I begin to train with some of the legions of Hollywood makeup artists who were using special cosmetic effects and techniques to assist burn survivors and other accident victims restore normalcy to their appearance.

After I acquired licensing in the field, I decided to establish a cosmetic rehabilitation practice of my own. A passenger on one of my last flights suggested the ideal location to me. A chance meeting with a stranger would end up making an enormous impact on the direction my career would take. He suggested I get an office in one of the largest medical buildings in the country that held the offices of three hundred physicians and dentists.

I followed his advice but it did not take long before the doctors objected to my presence in their building. Fortunately, the building was privately owned by a man who had suffered from acne all of his adolescent life and who had battled with the stigma of the scars from this horribly disfiguring disease. He allowed me to stay and I went on to gain the support and endorsement of the medical community for the next fifteen years.

Wright

How did you end up as a faculty associate and director of your own clinic?

Rayner

After six years of working with a wide spectrum of physicians and their patients I approached the University of California. I chose dermatology because so many dermatologic conditions are disfiguring. I knew a clinic in this hospital would be of great service to the community.

It was difficult at first to convince the doctors because they were unwilling to accept the concept from a non-health provider they perceived as ambitious and overly aggressive. I had to make it a community issue to convince them, so I appealed to the Department of Health and the media. It took about a year and a half but I really believed in the effort so I refused to let up; finally they conceded. I volunteered for the next four years before I was offered a faculty appointment.

Wright

What in your opinion was one of the hardest pressures you have had to face and how do you feel you were able to get past it?

Rayner

I was asked by the university to publish the first textbook on my specialty. I was terrified because I had no previous experience with writing and I could not even type. I had to sell the idea to a publisher first and that was accomplished instantly because I was very enthusiastic and the idea was novel. I did not understand the publishing world and as a result I overcame barriers because I simply was ignorant about all that it required to become an author. I was determined to do whatever it took to write this book and make it a teaching aid in the arts and in medicine.

The effort took four years. I had many setbacks and I discovered that there were books on practically every topic except the one I had chosen, which forced me to write on both medicine and esthetics simultaneously. To ensure that the textbook was scientifically correct and would be reviewed and endorsed by the medical journals, I approached the most highly respected physicians from multiple specialties that I could find and asked them to write the forward for every chapter. The book is still as relevant today as it was when I wrote it and has yet to be revised.

Wright

How did you begin your speaking career?

Rayner

I was asked to speak at medical conferences about the medical sub-specialty I had created and I was able to reach attending physicians and residents at other universities all over the country. I was invited to speak outside of the United States to give presentations and demonstrations. I traveled to Europe, to the Middle East, and went all the way to Eskisehir, Turkey.

At the same time I started to lecture I discovered I really enjoyed writing and I authored another book on woman's issues titled, *A Survival Guide for Today's Career Woman.*

I was interviewed on over fifty talk shows—amazingly enough, mostly by male callers who just wanted to understand women, their lives and their way of thinking. That is when I decided to give classes through the Learning Annex on "How Women Think and How to Develop Charisma." For the next six years I taught these courses twice a month.

Wright
When did you become an educator?

Rayner
One of the four clinics I established and staffed in teaching hospitals was located at San Francisco General Hospital at the height of the Aids Epidemic. I would work with AIDS patients helping them to cope with the stigma of the purplish lesions called Kaposi's sarcomas that erupted with the disease.

One of my professional mentors was a school owner who became ill and died from the disease. On his deathbed he made me promise I would share my knowledge with others. It was my commitment to him that led to obtain my teaching certifications. I wanted my graduates to be well regarded by the medical profession and to be viewed as associates, so I sought certification status for my institutes through the Board of Registered Nursing and the Department of Vocational Rehabilitation and the Cosmetology Board.

After teaching for eighteen years I had a bout with cancer and I retreated to the Caribbean for a year where I started to write distance education studies for specialized certification on subjects pertaining to wellness and esthetic patient care.

Wright
How did you end up in Washington, D.C., and become the Honorary Chairman for the Business Advisory Counsel?

Rayner
I married a French embassy chef who was recruited to Washington, D.C. Married to a chef I had plenty of time to devote to my passion and so I became a regular contributor to medical journals and professional industry publications. I wrote about many topics and discovered I enjoyed writing mainly about income development.

I decided to establish a second institute for career advancement on the East Coast and begin a seven-year effort to create comprehensive and relevant business development and marketing programs comparable to university courses but in home-study format that would be extremely affordable. After 9/11 there was a real need for training through distance education and my programs were ready and available.

What has made the training programs unique is the interaction that our students have weekly with the career coaches and private tutors we personally assign to each of them and our five-year commitment to continue to build and grow their careers in medicine and in the world of business and commerce.

Wright

How did you end up at the Humanities and Social Science Division of the Library of Congress?

Rayner

Ageism is an injustice that has greatly disturbed me for many years. I find it horrific the way older workers are treated after a certain age. Too many mature professionals are left out and struggle to support themselves. All of the educational programs I have written were with the Baby Boomers in mind. I wanted to be able to provide a means for them to recycle themselves back into the workforce as consultants to help them reinforce their retirement funds and to provide extra revenue for their health care by creating new income opportunities. That is how I ended up with my assignment at the Library of Congress research facility in the Humanities and Social Sciences Division.

Wright

What made you decide to write the very first continuing education business series on-line for the American Medical Woman's Association for CME credits?

Rayner

After I was asked by Congressman Tom Reynolds of New Jersey to be the Honorary Chairman of the Business Advisory Council in our nation's capital I realized that I had an obligation to apply my business skills and experience to aid in the health care crisis that we are all facing today.

As a Baby Boomer I fear a shortage of doctors as I age and clearly we will all be in serious trouble when so much of the population starts demanding the attention of the medical community in massive numbers. It amazes me how little is being done for our physicians. After all the opportunities I have been given by the medical community I am so thrilled to be able to assist them at a time when they are in need.

Wright

What in your opinion is the key to your success? And what course of action would you advise others to pursue if they wish to fully recognize their own ambitions?

Rayner

I believe the key to my success has been the decision I made early on to pursue my interests at all costs and to engage in so many fulfilling groundbreaking projects. I also think that it was my unwavering dedication to meet the expectations of those who gave me a chance because they recognized my capabilities and efforts. I would have done anything I could to not let them down and that's what I did.

My advice is to always be true to your innermost desires but to be mindful of your affect on others. Feed your intellect and follow your heart, but consider how you can make yourself the most useful.

About the Author

VICTORIA L. RAYNER is the author of books on skin health and woman's issues and she is a columnist who writes on issues related to business and career development. She was the first to pioneer distance learning CEU course content for clinically-focused skin care specialists, registered nurses and physicians and special training for the care of patients with serious appearance challenges. A certified instructor, Rayner established four cosmetic rehabilitation clinics and the Center for Appearance and Esteem in San Francisco, California (in 1981) and in Washington, D.C., the Rayner Institute for Career Advancement (in 2000). Rayner is currently working on the final draft of *Esthetic Intelligence: The Analytic Evolution of Cosmetic Patient Care*© and she is revising her book *Clinical Cosmetology: A Medical Approach to Esthetic Procedures.*

Victoria L. Rayner
Rayner Institute For Career Advancement
THE Willard Blvd. 1455 Pennsylvania Ave.
Ste. 100 on Fountain Plaza
Washington, D.C. 20004
Phone: 415.398.6013

Chapter 2

JIM ROHN

THE INTERVIEW

David E. Wright (Wright)

It's my sincere pleasure today to welcome Jim Rohn to *Rising to the Top.* Jim has helped motivate and train an entire generation of personal development trainers, as well as hundreds of executives from America's top corporations. He's been described as everything from "master motivator" to a "modern day Will Rodgers," to a legend. Jim has been internationally hailed over the years as one of the most influential thinkers of our time. His professional development seminars have spanned thirty-nine years. He has addressed over six thousand audiences and four million people worldwide. He has authored seventeen different books as well as dozens of audio and video programs. There simply are not enough superlatives when introducing Jim Rohn.

Jim, thank you for taking time to visit with us today.

Jim Rohn (Rohn)
Hey, my pleasure.

Wright
Before we dive into some pretty deep subjects, I know our readers would appreciate an update on your current focus.

Rohn
Well, I'm still involved in world travel—from Asia to South Africa, South America, to Europe, across the United States—which I've been doing for the last forty years and enjoying it very much.

Wright
I've belonged to a political discussion group called Great Decisions, for the last fifteen years. Every year we discuss conditions in Africa and every year we come away with our hands in our pockets, saying we don't know what can be done about it. Is it as bad as we believe?

Rohn
It's a complex continent and who knows what it will finally take. You know, there are some good signs but you're right.

Wright
The problems are just voluminous.

Rohn
I have lectured in all the major cities in South Africa. I've gone there several times over the last twenty years. When I first went they still had Apartheid, now that's all gone. There are some good signs that recovery is under way and I love to see that.

I first lectured in Moscow in Russia, starting about ten years ago and fortunately that was after the walls came tumbling down—they were changing from communism to capitalism. I've made about five lecture tours in Russia in the last ten years, teaching capitalism and personal responsibility and entrepreneurship. It's exciting to go back and see so many of them doing it. They still have a long way to go—there's still push and pull between the old ways and the new ways.

Years and years ago when I went to South America, every country had a dictator. Now they're all gone, for the most part. So there are a lot of improvements that have been made around the world but there is still a long way to go.

Wright

Do you appreciate the United States when you come back in?

Rohn

No doubt about it. This is the place where you can start with so little and still you can start with pennies and make your fortune with some good advice and coaching and a bit of training and personal responsibility and a whole lot of courage. That's extraordinary.

Wright

I spend a lot of time with professionals from all types of industries and I often give career advice when I'm asked.

Would you mind looking back over your career and sharing a story or two that demonstrates some relevant success principles? In other words, to what do you attribute your success in life?

Rohn

I met someone when I was twenty-five; his name was Earl Schoff (this is in most of my recordings and writings). I worked for him for five years. He died at the early age of forty-nine, but during those five years I worked for him, he gave me really a lot of the fundamentals—especially the economic and personal development principles—that revolutionized my life.

When I met him I had only pennies in my pocket, nothing in the bank, and creditors calling once in a while saying, "You told us the check was in the mail." That embarrasses me.

I think what triggered my search to find him was what I call "the Girl Scout story." I was at home alone and heard a knock on my door. I go to the door and there's this Girl Scout selling cookies. She gives me this great presentation (it's the best organization in the world). She goes on and on and she describes the several different flavors available and that the cost is only two dollars. Then she politely asked me to buy.

No problem, I wanted to buy—big problem, I didn't have two dollars. I can remember today that embarrassing moment—I'm a grown man and I'm twenty-five years old; I've had one year of college, I've got a little family started, I live in America, and I don't have two dollars in my pocket.

I didn't want to tell her that, so I lied to her and said, "Hey look, we've already bought lots of Girl Scout cookies, we've still got plenty in the house we haven't eaten yet.She said, "Oh, that's wonderful! Thank you very much," and she leaves.

When she leaves, I say to myself, "I don't want to live like this anymore. I mean how low you can get, lying to a Girl Scout? That's got to be the bottom, right?

I called it "the day that turns your life around." Everybody can look back at some of those days when you made a unique decision at a particular time and you were never the same again. That was one of those days.

Shortly after that I met this incredible mentor I went to work for—Earl Schoff. Using the things he taught me, I became a millionaire by the age of thirty-two.

It doesn't take much if you get the right information and put it to work and are willing to accept refinement, keep up your studies, and engage primarily in what we call "personal development"—becoming more valuable. For economics, personal development makes you more valuable to the marketplace. Personal development also makes you become more valuable as a father, a mother, a parent, a friend, a business colleague, and as a citizen.

Personal development is the subject I have talked most about seeing how valuable you can be to yourself, to your community, and to those around you.

I've got a little economic phase I use that says, "We get paid for bringing value to the marketplace." And the first part of that is the value you bring such as a product, but the biggest part of what you bring is how valuable you become through personal development. I say, "To climb the ladder of success, work harder on yourself than you do on your job." If you work hard on your job, you can make a living, if you work hard on yourself, you can make a fortune.

I learned those very fundamental ideas when I was twenty-five. Fortunately I discovered them at twenty-five rather than at fifty-five. Fifty-five is okay and seventy-five is still okay but gosh, it's good to learn them at the age of twenty-five when you can really put them to work. These ideas revolutionized my life and they formed the foundation of what I've shared now all these years in so many forms.

Wright

I've only heard the name Schoff twice. You just mentioned it and when I was in junior high school in seventh and eighth and ninth grades, one of my mentors was a coach named Schoff. He was a real mentor. This guy was just a fine, fine, man.

Rohn

The same man, Earl Schoff, influenced Mary Kay (the lady who started Mary Kay Cosmetics) and me back in 1955–1956. Those were the early, early years. Mary Kay went on to become a superstar. What he shared with me just transformed my life.

Wright

You're known throughout the world as a personal development expert. In practical terms what does that really mean?

Rohn

Well, there's a phase that says, "Success is not something you pursue, success is something you attract"—by becoming an attractive person. Currently I'm sharing it like this: to really do well you need multiple skills. If you've just got one skill, it's too risky economically. For example, a guy has worked for a company for twenty years and the division he works for goes out of business. He's lost his job and he tells us he's in financial trouble. The reason is that, even after twenty years of working, he only had one skill. If he had taken an accounting course or some other course two nights a week he would have had another skill to market. There's so much available out there that can increase your value to the marketplace.

I started learning these extra skills: finding good people, sales, finding a product I could believe in, and talk about its merits until somebody said Yes, follow up, and get referrals. Then I learned to build an organization. I then learned organization—getting people to work together. I needed to learn to get a team and work together. Then I learned recognition—I learned to reward people for small steps of progress.

The biggest skill I learned was communication. I got involved in training, showing people how the job works, and then I got involved in teaching. I taught setting goals, personal development leadership, and communication skills. My theme for that was, "You need both job skills and life skills," because just learning how to set goals revolutionized my life.

Then the ultimate in communication is learning to inspire—helping people see themselves as better than they are, transport them in to the future, paint the possibilities, and then use your own testimony. Say, "Hey if I can do it, you can do it."

So you're starting with pennies, you're behind, the creditors are calling; but that's not really what's important. What's important is the decision today to start the journey of self-improvement. I think that theme has been paramount in all of my teaching and training during the last forty years—work harder on yourself than you do on your job.

In leadership, I teach that to attract attractive people, you must be attractive. So it's a constant pursuit of self-development and personal development.

The theme during my career, teaching and training during the past forty years is: communication, managing your time, managing your money, and learning to inspire.

Wright

You know, I have my own opinion about how difficult it is for people to change whether it involves a health issue or dieting, for example. Do you believe that people can really change and why is change so difficult?

Rohn

Give easy steps. For example, if you want to change your health and you say, "I've got to do something that will make me healthy. My momma taught that an apple a day was healthy," why not start there?

If you don't start with something simple, you can forget the rest of the complicated stuff. Sometimes it's good to do it with someone else. I've found in all my entrepreneurial business projects during the last forty years, it's more inspiring to say, "Let's go do it," than to say, "I'm going to go do it." Get together with someone and say, "Let's get healthy, let's exercise, let's go to the gym, let's climb a mountain." The "let's" is what's very powerful. A lot of things are pretty tough to do all by yourself.

Wright

In the past there've been some major scandals in corporate America. I know you've counseled many high profiled executives over the years. Is there a leadership crisis in America? What do you think has contributed to this kind of moral failure?

Rohn

No, it's always been such from the beginning of recorded history, when there were just four people on earth. You know there was the great scandal of brother who killed brother (Cain and Abel). So it's not a current phenomenon—it's not a twenty-first century phenomenon. Even the Old Testament records good kings and bad kings—those who "did right in the sight of the Lord" and those who led the people into idolatry. You know, it's just not unusual.

My best explanation is the great adventure started back according to the Storyteller. God created all these angels and then gave them the dignity of choice, and a third of them decided to go with Lucifer and make a run on God's throne. They didn't win but it started what I call "the adventure of the Creator and the spoiler." And then I further describe it with the concept that the adventure of our life seems to be that opposites are in conflict and we are in the middle. But this is what makes a great adventure.

Illness tries to overcome your health, but if you work on your health you can overcome your illness. If, however, you let up the least little bit, sure enough, illness creeps up and takes away some more of your health.

Regarding liberty and tyranny in the world, for a while there was more tyranny than liberty. Since the walls came down in Berlin I am hopeful that there will be more liberty than tyranny in the future.

But whether its politics or whether it's corporations, it doesn't matter, the temptation is always there—the drama is always there. Should we do the right thing or would it be okay to cross the line? I use the following illustration sometimes: When I was a little kid I saw a cartoon of a little boy. The little boy had an angel—a little angel—on one shoulder, and a little devil on the other shoulder. Both of them were whispering in his ear. The little devil said, "Go ahead and do it, it will be okay."

The little angels says, "No, no, it *won't* be okay."

The little devil says, "Yes, yes, go ahead, it's okay; nobody will know."

The little angel says, "No, no, no!"

That little cartoon appeared back when I was a kid. It describes the concept of opposites in conflict and that's what makes an adventure.

There wouldn't be positive without negative it doesn't seem like. And you couldn't win if you couldn't lose. If you took a football today and walked out to the stadium and we followed you and in the football stadium you took the football and walked across the goal line, would we all cheer and call it a touchdown? The answer is No, that's silly. It's not a touchdown until you face the three-hundred-pounders. If you can muscle past them (they want to smash your face in the dirt) and if you can dance by the secondary, on a special day, we call it a touchdown, and maybe you win the championship.

That's the deal—opposites are in conflict. We're tempted every day, whether it's the little things or something big and major. You come to the intersection and the light is yellow and it starts to turn red. Some little voice may whisper to you, "Go ahead, you're late—you can make it." But if you try running that light you may wind up dead. If you say, "No, I'll be more cautious, then you live a little bit longer."

So it's not that we're not involved in this push and pull. It happens at the high echelons of corporate America. Little voices whisper in a collective way around the boardroom, and the board members decide to cross the line. They think, "It looks like we can get by with it—we can put it off shore or we can play some games here and we'll be okay" or "If we want this stock to grow and necessity demands it, we probably skate the line a little bit." That happens in the poorest of homes and it happens in the riches of homes. It happens in the boardroom and it happens on Main Street and it happens in the back alley. So it doesn't really matter where it is, temptation is always there. But that's what makes the adventure—to see if you can handle the temptation and do more right than wrong—have a longer list of virtues than mistakes—then you win.

Wright

I recently read an article you wrote about attitude. In it you said attitude determines how much of the future we're allowed to see. This is a fascinating thing to say. Will you elaborate on this thought?

Rohn

Well, it's attitude about four things:

1. *How you feel about the past.* Some people carry the past around like a burden. They continually live and dwell on their past mistakes. They live in the past (i.e., their past failures) and it just drains away all the energy they could apply to something much more positive. We have to have a good healthy attitude about the past. The key on that is just to learn from it. Hey, here's where I messed up, I've got that corrected now, and I'm going to make the changes for the future. We call that "drawing on the past" as a good school of experience to make corrections in errors in judgment or whatever put you in a bad place.

2. *How you feel about the future.* We need to look back for experience but we need to look ahead for inspiration. We need to be inspired by the goals we set for ourselves and for our family, the goals we've set for friendship, lifestyle, becoming wealthy, powerful, and influential, and as a unique citizen, those goals that get us up early and keep us up late, fire up the fuel of our imagination, and how can we accomplish them.

3. *How you feel about everybody.* You can't succeed by yourself. It takes everybody for each of us to be successful. Each of us needs all of us. One person doesn't make an economy; one person doesn't make a symphony orchestra. So you have to have that unique sense of the value of everybody and that it really does take everybody for any one person to be successful.

4. *How you feel about yourself.* This is the most important one. At the end of the day evaluate yourself: "I pushed it to the limit, I did everything I could, I made every call, I stretched as far as I could." If that's true, then you can lie down and sleep a good sleep. Solomon wrote, "The sleep of the laboring man is sweet . . ." (Ecclesiastes 5:12). This describes people who put in the work—who work hard either with their hands or with their mind or with their ability to communicate, whatever it is—so at the end of the day they feel good about themselves. Nothing is more powerful than high self-esteem. It builds self-confidence, which builds success.

Those five attitudes really do give you a promising look at the future. But if you're always being pulled back by the past or distracted because you find it difficult to manage your life with people you have to associate with, that's tough. And the better you can handle that and realize the law of averages says you're going to be around some good people and some bad people, and you're going to be around some ambitious people and some not so ambitious, the better off you'll be. You've got to learn to take it all in stride.

Then knowing that you're on track for better health and you're on track for becoming financially independent. You haven't quite got it solved, but you're on track for the management of your time and your money. And your attitude toward that really creates high inspiration that the future's going to multiply several times better than the past.

Wright

I don't normally like to frame a question in the negative but I thought it would be interesting to get your prospective on mistakes that people make in life and in business. If you had to name the top three on a list of mistakes people make that kept them from succeeding or living a fulfilled life, what would they be?

Rohn

Well, number one mistake economically is not to understand that people can make you wealthy. And all you have to do is just figure out how to do that. For example: Johnny mows Mrs. Brown's lawn and she pays five dollars. One day it occurs to him, "If I get my friend Paul to mow this lawn, Mrs. Brown would pay five dollars. I would give Paul four dollars and keep one for myself because I got the job." Instantly Johnny has now moved to a higher level of economics that says this is how you become wealthy.

A little phrase that philosophically and economically changed my life is: "Profits are better than wages." Wages make you a living but profits make you a fortune. You don't have to be General Motors, you don't have to be high in the industrial complex society to understand this concept; that's why it's so powerful to teach capitalism, how to buy and sell and how to sell and buy.

I've got so many stories of people I've helped in my seminars who started with pennies and now they're rich. That's the key—learning how to employ other people. First do it yourself—learn how to do it yourself—then find a need someone has and get someone else to render the service, and then someone else and then someone else. Teach them the same, and the principles of economics and capitalism. The knowledge of how to go from having pennies to gaining a fortune is so simple.

When I taught it to the Russians they couldn't believe how simple it was. I said, "Capital is any value you set aside to be invested in an enterprise that brings value to the marketplace hoping to make a profit"—that's capitalism. They couldn't believe I could put it in one sentence.

Wright

I can't either.

Rohn

I teach kids how to have two bicycles—one to ride and one to rent. It doesn't take long to make a profit. If you're halfway bright, if you get just a little advice to give you a chance to start, you'll make it.

I see capitalism in two parts—one is capital time, the other is capital money. If you wisely learn to invest capital money you can make a fortune. And then together with that, if you can learn to invest capital time you can also amass a fortune. You set aside time to be invested in an enterprise.

I started that part-time when I was twenty-five years old, all those years ago in 1955. I took about fifteen to twenty hours a week part-time and invested it in a capital enterprise. By the time I was thirty-two I was a millionaire. It didn't take much money because I only invested $200, which I borrowed. That was my capital money, but the other was my capital time. Once I learned how to invest both and then learned how to teach and train and inspire other people to do the same, it totally changed my life.

I don't have to worry about social security—I developed my own social security. It's interesting that they're not teaching that today when social security is such a main topic. We've got to let our young people put aside some of that withholding and put it in a personal account. How about teaching them how to be financially independent? Who's doing that? John Kennedy said," Don't ask what your country can do for you . . ." Don't ask what the social security program can do for you . . . Why not ask what you can do for your country—or social security? Could I mow Mrs. Brown's lawn and collect five dollars and do it part-time? Then could I get someone else to do it and then someone else to do another job, and finally work my way from the pennies in my pocket to the fortune that I could have because this is America—the land of opportunity?

It's startling how simple it is in concept and how really easy it is in practice; but the results can be phenomenal. I got such great early results that I never did look back, from age twenty-five until today.

For me it's fun to teach it. I've been teaching it now for all these years and I've got some testimonials where I helped people start, just like I started with pennies and now they're rich. It's just exciting.

One of the great exciting experiences is to have your name appear in somebody's testimonial: "Here's the person who found me, here's the person who taught me, here's the person who wouldn't let me quit, gave me more reasons for staying than for leaving. Here's the person who believed in me until I could believe in myself," then they mention your name. I call that big time, and you can't buy it with money. You have to simply earn it by sharing ideas with somebody that makes a difference in their life. And I love to do it.

Wright
This is the definition of great mentors.

Rohn
Yes, I love to be that. Hopefully my books and tapes and my personal appearances have done that during the last forty years.

Wright
I'd like to go back to the issue of personal development and change. Considering the issues most Americans face in this modern era with all of our technology, where would you advise most people to focus their energy if they could only change one thing about themselves?

Rohn
I'd advise them to start figuring out to how to learn another skill, and then another skill. Then it would be good to learn another language. People who know more than one language receive good pay. Some of my business colleagues who speak three or four languages make three or four million a year. Not that this is a guarantee, but that's just an idea for self-improvement. Learn something beyond what you know now because it could be something that you can cash in on, maybe sooner than you think.

Wright
Not to mention the fact that you're talking for the first time to another whole culture and look what you could learn. I've always been fascinated by the Chinese culture.

Rohn
I would also suggest that people develop wise use of their time and then wise use of their money. I teach kids to not spend more than seventy cents out of every dollar—ten cents for charity or church, ten cents for active capital (i.e., the two bicycles, one to ride and one to rent concept), then passive capital of 10 percent. Let someone else use it (you provide the capital that will pay you dividends, increase in stock or whatever). I call it "seventy-ten-ten and ten." Then I teach

not to buy the second car until you've bought the second house. Cars won't make you rich but houses will make you rich. I love to teach that.

A lady called me from Mexico not long ago and said, "Mr. Rohn, I'm now shopping for my third car because I just finished paying for my third house." She started listening to my training ten years ago. She not only uses it, she teaches it. Down in Mexico she makes about $40,000 a month, which down there is just staggering.

But it's fun—it's been fun for me over the years to have stories like that. I use my own story as an inspiration not only for myself but also for the people who listen to my lectures. And then it's fun to watch people actually grab hold of something and turn it into success.

Wright

Jim, it's been a sincere joy having this enlightening conversation with you today. I really appreciate and thank you so much again for taking the time to be with us on *Rising to the Top*.

Rohn

I appreciate it and I thank you for calling.

Wright

Thank you so much.

About the Author

Jim Rohn is a philosopher, motivational counselor, business executive, and best-selling author. He has been recognized as the greatest motivational speaker of all time. He is one of the world's most sought-after success counselors and business philosophers. Some of his most thought-provoking topics include: sales and entrepreneurial skills, leadership, sales and marketing, success, and personal development.

Jim Rohn has conducted seminars for over thirty-nine years and addressed over six thousand audiences and four million people worldwide. He is a recipient of the 1985 National Speakers Association CPAE Award. He's authored over seventeen different books, audio, and video programs. Rohn has been internationally hailed over the years as one of the most influential thinkers of our time.

Revealing contemporary success secrets in a way that is both accessible and practical, Jim ignites enthusiasm and a can-do attitude in all who hear him speak. He approaches the subjects of personal and professional success by asking four questions: Why? Why not? Why not you? Why not now? He answers these questions and reveals practical, perceptive secrets for success and productivity. His special style, laced with witticisms and anecdotes, captivates listeners. Among his most thought-provoking topics are: sales and entrepreneurial skills, leadership, sales and marketing, success, and personal development.

Jim Rohn
www.jimrohn.com

Chapter 3

KEN RASNER

David Wright (Wright)

Today we are talking with Ken Rasner. Ken is a member of the National Speakers Association and author of *The Prosperity Architect.* He gives seminars and teaches workshops all over the world and is considered an expert in the field of wealth creation for the average person. He was on the faculty at a major university in Southern California and has been a guest speaker at businesses and universities worldwide. Ken is CEO of BioStreams International. He is also President of Harmonic Marketing and CEO of Seven Greatest Secrets.com.

Ken, welcome to *Rising to the Top: A Guide to Success.*

Rasner

Thank you David; I'm very happy to be here.

Wright

Ken, you spend a lot of your time giving free seminars helping people create what you refer to as "massive wealth." You seem passionate about it. Will you tell us about this passion of yours?

Rasner

I'd love to David; but first, let me tell you that I'm excited to be part of this book, *Rising to the Top: A Guide to Success*. I believe we can all "rise to the top," we just need to have the sincere desire to do it, know what to do, and then actually do it. As we rise to the top, money is not the only measure of success, but it is a large part of the equation.

You're right, I am passionate about helping people create wealth and I'll tell you why. In our world today it's getting more and more difficult to break even. Every time many people catch a break, the price of homes or the price of cars or groceries or the price of gas goes through the roof and the "break" just keeps them even. We're not supposed to just get by—we're supposed to get ahead. We were not born to struggle.

I give free seminars for two reasons: First, I really want to help everybody and when it costs money to attend, some people won't be able to come. I want to help good people live in abundance. I believe that money amplifies a person. What I mean by that is that if you are a good person, money will make you better; it just makes it easier for you to continue to do good things. I want to help people do better financially, so at the free seminars we explain the basics of creating wealth. Good people usually share their wealth and help those who are less fortunate. Unfortunately, since money amplifies a person, if you are a bad person, money will make you worse. So if that's you, please don't ever attend one of our Prosperity Architect Seminars.

The second reason I give free seminars is that we're looking for people who are excited about creating massive wealth and want to take the next step. We encourage them to go beyond the seminar and attend a Prosperity Weekend Workshop.

Wright

So tell us about these Prosperity Workshops. What makes them unique? What is it that you do there?

Rasner

Our workshops have a strong focus on maximizing the financial prosperity of each individual. And we work to make that happen quickly. We know that for many people in today's world, money is not always as abundant as they would like. Most people want to make more money and they need it to happen quickly, they just don't know exactly how to do it. At the workshops we not only show them how, we help them do it, starting with who they are, where they are and with what they already have. A lot of people question whether they can create wealth. Once they attend the Prosperity Architect Workshop they get excited as massive wealth creation becomes a reality for them.

I always make sure that those attending the workshop understand that to be truly prosperous you have to have more than money. And these intangibles need to be sought at the same time. Don't pursue money with the idea that "once I'm rich then I'll worry about the real values of life." Those who do that miss the value and fullness of being prosperous. Besides, a huge part of creating wealth is about your mindset and your energy, so with the wrong approach, the money won't come anyway. I will tell you that your spiritual relationship, your family relationships, lasting true friendships, and your health are all easily the most important things you will ever have. Money just makes sharing all those things easier and more fun.

Wright

There are other wealth-building workshops, why is your program so successful for the average person?

Rasner

It's really only two things: first it's the method of learning the Seven Greatest Secrets. We clearly explain *why* the Principle of Prosperity works. Then, in terms everyone can understand, we even explain *how* the quantum physics theories apply to rapidly creating and accepting massive wealth.

Next, we work though each of the Seven Greatest Secrets of Prosperity step by step. We actually lay the complete foundation for each individual right there. The key is that as we expose each of the secrets, *we practice them and apply them with the individuals in attendance to their specific situation.* We keep our workshops small so we can give participants lots of individual attention.

Using this individualized approach, the Principle of Prosperity is really easy to understand and the steps are actually easy to do. In fact, by the end of the workshop, you can't help but continue with them. And these secrets absolutely can lead to massive prosperity for everyone.

The second thing that is unique about the Prosperity Architect Workshops is the tremendous follow-up that helps every individual reach his or her personal vision of prosperity. In other words, the prosperity students don't just show up and then at the end of the weekend hear "thank you, goodbye, and good luck"—everyone is part of the workshop extension.

Wright

That sounds great. I like the idea of individual focus.

Tell us what you mean by the term "workshop extension."

Rasner

David, recently a lot of people have seen the movie or read the book called *The Secret.* The message in the book is not new. In fact, it's been around a long time; it's just that this book has taken the concept to the masses as never before. Unfortunately, often people will watch the movie or read this book or any book on creating wealth, get the general idea, and then expect miracles. When miracles don't happen, they blame others and doubt the integrity of the concept, the system, or the program and figure they aren't supposed to be rich anyway.

As I mentioned, our Prosperity Architect Workshop is two full days of intensive training. During those two days, as we push the Universal Law of Attraction to the limit, we focus specifically on creating massive wealth. But then comes the workshop extension. *Every* student is worked with weekly, sometimes daily, long after the workshop is completed. That consistent follow-up helps them stay connected, helps them maximize their vision of wealth, and helps them stay committed.

We make sure that someone doesn't come to a workshop and waste time and money. I've met too many people who have gone to a wealth-building program of some kind only to say that it was really good, but they didn't do anything with what they learned. Why does that happen? It happens because once you leave a workshop, a lot of what was covered seems to run together. If you didn't get very well organized during the workshop and you didn't actually get started on each phase of success; if you don't have anyone to talk to, ask questions of, and to actually work with you individually, then applying the things you learned, even though it's not extremely difficult, causes most people to give up. We don't let that happen.

Here's a summary: We know most people want more money, and *most people will jump at a chance to spend a weekend with experts* who will take the time to show them exactly how to get it. The Prosperity Architect Workshop is a weekend devoted to the thorough understanding of the proven secrets of getting rich. Then those secrets are individually applied, right there during the weekend. Everyone there actually goes through the process of setting wealth creation into motion for their personal lives. They also receive the tools *and help* to continue and make it become a reality!

Wright

With that kind of personalized follow-through, I can understand why your workshop attendees become successful. Have many of your students done well?

Rasner

I've been blessed and have been able to help many people raise their financial status significantly and quickly. I've assisted and coached several people who have become millionaires. A few others have become multi-millionaires.

I was blessed to coach a man who four years ago was out of work. He had a vision and he began to practice the Seven Greatest Secrets of Prosperity, and today he's worth over thirty million dollars.

But it's not always about the millions. Sometimes it's just about getting more out of life, and sometimes it's about just getting back to ground zero—finally breaking even and now beginning to move ahead.

I've helped several who have struggled most of their life. Many of those people have now raised their income to $8,000 to $10,000 a month. And in many other cases people have started receiving checks of up to $12,000 to $15,000 *a week*. Now they're doing what they really want to do and they have more time to enjoy their family. What they're doing, you can also do, and you can do it with who you are, where you are, and with what you already have.

Let me tell you about Rodney. Rodney owned a very profitable business with his wife of twenty-four years, Michelle. In less than two years, Rodney lost his sister and two brothers. The day after his brother's funeral, his mother died. Six months later, his wife died of cancer. Rodney's life was a mess. He had lost his business, he lost his home, and he lost his car. Can you imagine how he must have felt? His sky seemed to always have dark clouds. He easily could have given up. He took odd jobs just trying to get by. He began living in a single rented room in a stranger's house and riding the bus to find better work. He wasn't making it. It sure would have been easy for him just to accept that life had dealt him a losing hand. Most people would have given up, stayed focused on, and wallowed in those negative events. And it would be hard to blame somebody for that response given the circumstances.

But that's not who Rod is. All his life he's focused on the positive things, trusted in God, and in himself. So he picked himself up and looked around for ways to take control of his today and his tomorrow. Four months ago Rodney learned The Seven Greatest Secrets of Prosperity and he began to practice them exactly as he was coached. Today he no longer lives in someone else's house. He has his own place. He has a very nice car and earns about $80,000 per year. And his income will easily double or triple in the next eight to twelve months! This has been accomplished from right where he was, with what he already had.

There are a lot of people in the same boat. They see other people getting rich. Much of the time these people are not special, they aren't any better looking, any more talented, and they're really not much smarter, yet they are becoming wealthy. Why is that? The answer is how every individual approaches wealth creation. That's why we teach it and practice it in the workshops. It's fun and the success has been staggering.

Wright

Tell me Ken, how did you become an expert in helping others become wealthy?

Rasner

To become an authority in any field, you have to thoroughly research and extensively study that field's current findings along with its foundation and its history. Then you need to meet and interview those who have obtained the pinnacle of the subject area and lastly you need to go personally do it. So, Learn it, Live it, Watch it, Study it, Prove it, Do it. Then you go on to teach others. When they become successful, you have the right to be considered an authority.

I began studying wealth creation, and I mean not just reading but studying and underlining and taking notes on hundreds of books. Concurrently I spent a massive amount of time and thousands of dollars on seminars and workshops. I've interviewed a dozen millionaires and one billionaire. And along the way I began to put into practice what I had learned. On my way to an income putting my family in the top one-half of 1 percent in the United States, I still made lots of mistakes, but I learned even more from those mistakes.

More and more I learned each piece of the puzzle. One major piece showed up consistently from every source and that is how critical your mindset and your attitude are. When you master your attitude and then focus your energy on the correct steps (the "secrets"), financial success is absolutely available to everyone.

Let me put it another way: I'm sure that as a child your parents (just like mine) said to you, "If you put your mind to it, you can do or be anything you want." And they were right! However, it's very important to note that they used two extremely important words: "if" and "mind."

Let me start with the word "mind." Over the last thirty years, as I attended those seminars and read all those books, I found that most of them focused on the incredible power of the mind. From the classic books such as *The Power of Positive Thinking, Think and Grow Rich,* and *The Science of Getting Rich* to the newer books like *Attractor Factor, The Secret,* and *Cracking the Millionaire Code,* they all talk about using your *mind* to attract and manifest success. Our brain is an amazing part of us. When used effectively we really can manifest into our lives anything we want.

Later I added visits to brain mapping centers and neurology departments of major universities, followed by exhaustive research in quantum physics. The total purpose of this was so that in my mind I could validate the manifestation theories with established scientific studies.

Next, I surrounded myself with extremely successful, brilliant people who had individually become exceptionally wealthy. Together we developed the very foundation of wealth creation using the mind as the basis. We began to put the Seven Greatest Secrets to the test and found through personal experience and from the success of our students that these methods work beyond our wildest dreams. We are now confident that we can help anyone who is coachable to become wealthy.

Wright

Okay, the second word you mentioned earlier is "if." That seems straightforward, so why is "if" such an important word?

Rasner

We all have the ability to become wealthy. We were not born to be poor or to struggle. I'm a Christian and I firmly believe that God wants us to have abundance. In Luke 16:11, the Bible explains that we will need to learn to handle earthly wealth: *"So if you have not been trustworthy in handling worldly wealth, who will trust you with true riches?"* What this is clearly saying is: become prosperous; prove that you can handle worldly wealth! In Genesis 24:35 we are reminded that wealth is a blessing of God: *"The Lord has blessed my master abundantly, and he has become wealthy."* In no way does that say anything other than God says it's okay to be wealthy.

The problem is that many people believe somehow that it's spiritual or noble to be poor. That just isn't true. It's okay to be rich. In fact, part of our job on this planet is to help others. I'm here to tell you that it's easier to help others when you have lots of money. *"As evening approached, there came a rich man from Arimathea, named Joseph, who had himself become a disciple of Jesus"* (Mathew 27:57).

Valerie and I are supporting a ministry and building an orphanage in the Philippines. Why there? Well, we did some missionary work there, not much but enough to see underprivileged kids, many without clothes, digging in the garbage dump every day looking for food to eat. That's not acceptable. No child should have to eat garbage! Being poor is not good. Sophie Tucker, Mae West, and Gertrude Stein all said it best when they said: "I've been rich and I've been poor and believe me, rich is better."

Do you want to help others? Become prosperous. Want to take care of family members? Become prosperous. Want more time with your family? Do you want to travel the world? Or retire your parents? Become prosperous. Do you want to help your church? Become prosperous. Do you want to do all of that and more? Become *very* prosperous! And guess what—you can, and, it's okay!

Success is a choice. We just have to choose to create that lifestyle for ourselves. We have to learn what to do, how to do it, and then go do it.

We have the ability to become wealthy; we know the secrets, so we know how to do it. The problem is that most people don't take the time to learn those secrets and when they do, they don't apply them.

Each of the Seven Greatest Secrets start with the right mindset—the right attitude. As we teach each of the secrets, we get the right attitude and we keep that mindset permanently.

Wright

You said that the seven secrets to creating wealth all start with the right attitude. How were you able to create your prosperity attitude?

Rasner

Well, David, to answer that completely, I'd like to tell you a little about my personal background.

When I was born, we had what was considered a lot of money for that time. Though I was only a few years old, I remember everyone making a big deal about the fact that my dad bought a new Cadillac loaded with extras. The big deal wasn't so much that he bought a new Caddie. It was that when he went to the dealership and picked out the car he wanted, he just reached into his pocket and pulled out thousands of dollars. He paid for the car in cash! Even today very few people have the liquidity to do that.

About two years later, one of the guys who was driving a truck for our company ran a stop sign and caused some extremely serious damage. Since my father didn't believe in insurance, but did believe in making everything whole, by the time he took care of the damages, we had lost everything. After that the family struggled financially and my father struggled emotionally. He began to drink heavily and eventually my mother and my brother, Larry, and I were on our own. My married sister, Barbara, helped us move from Illinois to Arizona where my oldest brother, Farrel, helped us find a place to live.

Farrel was only twenty-two at the time and had a family of his own to support, so everyone pitched in. Each of my two oldest brothers, Farrel and Reggie, and my sister sent us a few dollars each month to help cover the $250 per month rent. My mother took any job she could get, from scrubbing floors to babysitting. We didn't know about welfare, though I doubt that my mom would have accepted it anyway. At first we lived in a trailer and then we got a small house.

As time went on things didn't change much. As I got older and began to attend high school I remember our circumstances clearly. Though we never let anyone know, there were times when we didn't have any water at the house, so we would "borrow" water from the neighbor's hose. We used that so we could brush our teeth and flush the toilets. Larry and I showered in the school locker room; I don't know what my mother did. Often we had no electricity in the house, so when it got dark we went to bed, when it got light we got up. When it got hot, we took off the bed covers, when it got cold we put more on. We had no transportation so we bummed rides from our friends or we walked everywhere. Some of our so-called "friends" who had their own car would drive right by us, ignoring us as we walked to school carrying our books, our band instruments, and other school supplies.

My mother made us "special" dinners and we thought they were great. There were many nights of macaroni and cheese and other nights of "tomato gravy dinners" (a dinner of hot tomato soup poured over bread that has been broken into pieces).

Wright

Not the ideal situation for growing up—

Rasner

I agree, but a lot of good came from it. My mother (Pauline Rasner), who turned ninety-three years old this year, bless her heart, never let us feel poor. We always felt as though we were fine. She kept the financial struggles to herself and always portrayed an attitude of success. What I mean by that is we always were dressed nicely and our clothes were washed and pressed.

She didn't want us to miss any school function. By my senior year in high school we had bought a used Chevy. It was in good shape, but you had to push it to get it started. Since we didn't have the money to fix the car, I surely didn't think about going to the school prom, and honestly, I was perfectly all right to skip it. But my mother would have none of that. She fashioned a corsage from flowers out of our flower bed and I put on my only sports coat, a hand-me-down from Larry. My date and I laughed as she (in her prom dress) and I pushed the car to get it started.

I'm the only kid I know who received a high school scholarship from the PTA to help pay for my graduation gown and senior picture.

So the reason I told you about my childhood is simple: we always lived as if we were prosperous—we inherited the attitude of success, even when we ate tomato gravy dinners.

Wright

The subtitle of your latest book is *The Seven Greatest Secrets To Rapidly Creating and Accepting Massive Wealth.* Would you explain what you mean by "accepting wealth"? Are there people who won't take the money if you offer it to them?

Rasner

Probably not, at least not that I'm aware of. I think if we go up to almost anyone and offer him or her massive amounts of money, almost everyone would ask what the catch is—then when the realization dawns that there's no catch, the person would take the money.

But we're not talking about handing money to someone; we're talking about creating it—creating it with being exactly who you are (for the most part, with your current education), being where you are (not having to move to any distant place), and with what you have. You see, often when people are working in a special way to create massive wealth and the money starts to come, what happens? A lot of people, in fact most of them, begin to unconsciously do things to stop the success. They sabotage themselves, not on purpose, but they just create obstacles that won't let the wealth continue.

Wright

Why would anyone do that? It seems to me that if it's working, don't fix it.

Rasner

I couldn't agree with you more, however, many people have negative subconscious feelings about being rich. They read in the Bible, "blessed are the poor in spirit" but all they hear is "blessed are the poor." They see wealthy people on television being portrayed as crooks or snobs or immoral and they definitely don't want any of that. Sometimes it's ingrained in our minds from the time we are little. Maybe we've heard someone say something like, "We may be poor but at least we're honest." That clearly implies that rich people are dishonest. Or, "Don't go over there son, those rich people don't want to be bothered with us." Many, many people just totally fear success, so they have developed a self-sabotaging, self-destructive mode that actually and without their being aware of it creates road blocks that stop them from becoming wealthy.

When I was helping one of my distant relatives, he was faced with the very real prospect of earning $70,000 a month. His initial response was, "I'll take it, but holy cow, what would I ever do with all that money?" Subconsciously he's already rejected that level of financial success.

So in your development, it's not only important to learn and then use the Principle of Prosperity to create wealth, you have to identify and overcome the self-made landmines in the financial self-destruct cycle. You have to break down the barriers that will unknowingly cause you fail, which in turn causes you to remain right where you are financially.

Wright

Ken, what is the most unexpected thing people learn as they experience the proper steps in wealth creation?

Rasner

I'm glad you asked because creating wealth will happen and after the first day pretty much everybody accepts that and expects it. People are leaving these workshops and are truly making major improvements in their financial situation. But what is really exciting is that when applying the secrets of the Prosperity Principle some great "side effects" show up and nobody really expects them.

Wright

Like what?

Rasner

To answer that, I need to explain a little about brain waves. Now I'm no expert, but I've studied a lot of articles and books and have met with and worked with experts from major universities, so what I'm telling you is based upon some of the latest research and clinical studies.

In addition to being biochemical, we are electromagnetic. At our fundamental core we are energy. Werner Heisenberg, a pioneer in quantum physics, implies that no particle ever comes to a complete stop. Due to its field of energy, it is constantly interacting with all subatomic matter. According to Lynne McTaggart, author of *The Field,* a field is a medium that connects various points in space though a force such as electromagnetism: "Simply put, a field is a region of influence." Many top physicists now believe that all elementary particles interact with each other. They exchange energy through quantum particles. Therefore, at our core we are constantly resonating with all things as we are connected to all other energy at that level.

Brainwave Mapping has *scientifically proven* that your mind produces frequencies or vibrations based upon your thoughts and emotions. The brain signal is divided into thirty-six different frequencies. Electroencephalograms (EEGs) are electrical signals obtained from electrodes placed on the head. These brain wave signals represent the state of cell activity in the brain. Twenty-four hours a day nerve cells in the brain are generating electrical impulses called brain waves. The brain patterns correlate with thoughts, emotions, and state of being. Like a tuning fork, we know that vibrations will attract and respond to like vibrations, good or bad. Whatever vibes you put out is what you will attract. The Universal Law of Attraction states that your strong vibrations will manifest themselves into reality. You can change the type of reality you attract and increase the amount that you attract simply by changing your mental vibrations. When you maximize the proper prosperity techniques, *money will flow to you*—and anyone can do it. You are meant to have abundance.

By learning the techniques that focus and amplify these brain wave frequencies, we can determine which vibrations we attract and therefore what we manifest in our lives. When we use the Principle of Prosperity techniques to focus our thoughts, energies, and emotions on positive prosperity outcomes, we will attract and manifest positive prosperity outcomes.

There are four categories of brain waves. They are: Beta, Alpha, Theta, and Delta, each representing an increasingly relaxed state of mind. At our workshop we teach proper meditation techniques. Now this is really only a minor part of the workshop, but it's extremely important.

I always thought of meditation as boring and pretty much meaningless. I pictured it as sitting with your legs crossed, your thumbs and fingers making a circle and interlocking your left and right hands while you hum. After three minutes I was thinking about lunch.

I was wrong. What is very exciting and interesting is that as you learn to meditate properly, you can learn to enter into these more relaxed and focused states of mind that can allow you to release some very beneficial, natural hormones. These hormones can actually reverse the aging process! Additionally, you get into a super creative mode and you begin to send out super positive, creative frequencies. So you could be "getting rich and getting younger" every day—now that's exciting!

Wright

Wow Ken, that's deep.

Rasner

I get carried away sometimes when talking about this because it is so exciting. There are clinical studies (one from the University of Wisconsin) showing that specific hormones can reverse the ageing process by as much as twenty years! It's truly so much fun to help people take control of their financial life, which usually gives them control of their time and often their total life. It's not hard to learn and it's not hard to do.

Wright

Well, I've certainly learned a lot and I've enjoyed talking with you.

Rasner

Thank you, David. I've really enjoyed being included as part of this awesome book. I hope each of our readers will "rise to the top"!

Wright

Today we've been talking with Ken Rasner. Ken is a member of the National Speakers Association, and author of *The Prosperity Architect.* He gives seminars and teaches workshops all over the world and is considered an authority on the techniques of creating wealth. He has taught at a major university in Southern California and has been a guest speaker at businesses and universities worldwide. Ken is CEO of BioStreams International. He is also President of Harmonic Marketing and CEO of Seven Greatest Secrets.com.

Ken, thank you so much for being with us today on *Rising to the Top: A Guide to Success.*

About the Author

KEN RASNER lives in Southern California with his wife, Valerie, who is an optometrist. They have two sons. His son, Robert, is a full-time professional magician (www.rasnermagic.com) who has also had success in multiple television shows, commercials, and films. Robert lives in Los Angeles. His son, Richard, lives in Las Vegas and is a professional photographer (www.nakayamastudios.com) at his studio, The Las Vegas Photo Center.

Ken Rasner is a member of the National Speakers Association, author of *Network Marketing 101: Back to the Basics,* co-author of *Speaking of Success*, and author of *The Prosperity Architect*. He gives seminars and teaches workshops all over the world and is considered an authority on the techniques of creating wealth. He has taught at a major university in Southern California and has been a guest speaker at businesses and universities worldwide. Ken is CEO of BioStreams International. He is also President of Harmonic Marketing and CEO of Seven Greatest Secrets.com.

Ken Rasner
5225 Canyon Crest Dr., Suite 71-620
Riverside, CA 92507
www.SevenGreatestSecrets.com

Chapter 4

Dr. Jan Northup

David Wright (Wright)

Dr. Jan Northup, president of Management Training Systems, Inc., is an internationally known author, speaker, organizational strategist, training specialist, and business coach. For the past twenty-five years, Jan has focused her efforts on working with senior leaders in both public and private organizations in the areas of organizational effectiveness and employee performance management through strategic planning facilitation, developing employee recruitment and retention processes, establishing employee mentoring programs, and conducting team building, conflict resolution, and communications training for employees. Jan has led organizations as they embraced change and moved to higher levels of innovation and tangible results.

Jan created "The Promotable Woman: What Makes The Difference" video training program that was featured on the Public Broadcasting Service. Close to a million people worldwide have attended her seminars, training classes, and presentations. She has been a featured speaker at numerous regional and national conferences and was the first woman to conduct a nationwide speaking tour of Australia on women's management issues. Dr. Northup's latest books, *Life's a Bitch and Then You Change Your Attitude: 5 Secrets of Taming Life's Roller Coaster and Building Resilience*, examines personal and organizational resilience.

Jan, welcome to *Rising to the Top: A Guide to Success*.

Dr. Jan Northup (Northup)

Thank you, David.

Wright

What is resilience? Is it a trait or characteristic with which we are born or do we learn resilience?

Northup

Let's start by defining resilience. Webster's dictionary defines resilience, in the noun form, as an ability to recover from, or adjust easily to misfortune or change. Resilient as an adjective is defined as being capable of withstanding shock without permanent deformation or rupture.

Now those are the formal definitions. In my research on the topic of resilience, I asked hundreds of people from all walks of life and from all levels in organizations for their definitions of resilience. I also asked them to share an experience when they consciously drew upon their resilience or in looking back on an experience where resilience played an important part. They gave definitions such as having a positive attitude, bouncing back, pulling themselves up by their bootstraps, and finally, hitting their head against the wall, falling down, getting up, and hitting their head against the wall again. But they kept moving in the direction they wanted to go. The most common or most frequent answer I got when I asked for a definition of resilience was, "I'm a survivor."

As we continue to research resilience, I think being a survivor is one thing but being resilient goes far beyond surviving. We all know people who have survived something. But if you just survived, it meant that you just barely made it through. You got to the other side of something that was unpleasant or something that didn't have the outcome you wanted. But if you have resilience, that means you moved beyond surviving and you moved forward learning from that experience. You then were better equipped to deal with life in the future because you made it through that situation.

Now to answer the second part of you question, "Is resilience a trait or a characteristic?" Studies vary. Some researchers will say that people are naturally born with resilience. Other researchers will say that everyone is born equal in their ability to be resilient but some develop strategies for becoming more resilient. Personally, I think it is a combination of both.

Most of us can think of someone who seems to have had resilience throughout his or her life. From the moment these people were born they seemed to bounce back, meet adversity head on, were able to adapt to changes, and were able to do it with a fair amount of ease.

Also we know people who have experienced situations in life where they struggled and didn't seem to know how to call upon their resilience. They were unable to move through change and unpleasant situations without experiencing stressful side effects. If they were able to recognize the need for resilience, they may have attended training classes, sought the advice of a counselor, found a mentor, or modeled the behaviors and attitudes of those they saw who were effectively dealing with adversity. They were searching for tools to help them maintain control of their emotions and reactions during difficult times.

Wright

Why is it important?

Northup

You need only to reflect on the rapid changes in our environment today, whether it is within our work environment or our personal environment, to understand the need to adapt to change and to understand the different areas where we experience change.

It has been found that the people who are most successful in adapting to change and moving with the ups and downs in their personal relationships and their work demonstrate a high degree of resilience. Even organizations that are successful in moving forward report that the resilience of individual employees is what helps them to move from one situation to the next with less negative impact on the workforce and the organization.

When we talk about the changes in our society, we are seeing rapid changes in our business world and global economy. People are changing jobs and careers quickly. It is estimated that people entering the workforce today will change jobs twenty or more times and will change career fields at least seven times during their work life.

In the past we may think of our parents who worked for what we called the gold watch. Those days are gone. According to the Department of Labor statistics, the number of U.S. workers in agriculture related jobs has dropped from 85 percent in the early 1900s to only 3 percent today. In the 1950s, 70 percent of U.S. workers were in production or manufacturing jobs. Now there are less than 15 percent. If we look at the job statistics for today, two thirds of all U.S. workers are in the service sector and eight out of ten of the fastest growing jobs are computer and technology related. This makes knowledge and people our most valued resources.

Resilience is a must. It is a personal and an organizational tool that will allow us to meet the constant changes in the workforce and changing technologies. We are also finding our family and our relationships structures have changed. We see combined families due to remarriage, same sex marriage, single parents, adult children returning home to live with their parents, and cohabitation to reduce financial burdens. We may need to call upon our resilience to help us make choices, help others accept our choices, and to accept the choices others have made. The key is to maintain that sense of who we are and what we can be as we set goals for our envisioned future.

Wright

If we have it, can we lose it? How do we learn resilience?

Northup

First, can we lose our resilience? You bet! We can lose resilience in a matter of seconds or over a long period of time, depending on the situation. You can probably think of a personal situation where everything was going along fine, life seemed to be a breeze, and then all of a sudden something happened and it took the wind out of you. It really was an affront to everything you thought would happen in your life. It challenged your values and you lost your resilience. On the other hand, you may have been in a situation where you just didn't know how you were going to cope or you didn't understand if you had the strength to go on. Then somewhere within you, you drew upon *something* that helped you get through the situation and helped you move on in a positive direction. We call that *something* resilience.

Wright

In the title, you mention five secrets to taming life's roller coaster. How is life like a roller coaster? That's an interesting image. Do we all have a roller coaster ride in life?

Northup

When I was a child, the roller coaster was my favorite amusement park ride. During my research and work with people over the last twenty-five years, I constantly heard about the ups and downs of life. It reminded me of the ups and downs on a roller coaster.

If you think back, have you ever ridden a roller coaster? You can imagine or recall the first time or the one hundredth time you rode a roller coaster. The anticipation as you buckled in, the cars moving slowly up the track, your wait for the rise to the top of the first large peak, and your anticipation of that impending and inevitable drop. Maybe the anticipation took your breath away. Maybe you were fearful but you held on with a death grip hoping that the seat belt (we'll loosely call it a seat belt), would hold you in. Then the car drops. Again, the feeling could have been total fear or there could have been an adrenalin rush that was so thrilling you actually loosened the death grip on the bar in front of you, held you hands in the air, and screamed at the top of your lungs as if you were defying all the gods of the world.

As I talked to people, I heard examples of how sometimes it was just a slow ride to the top but then they reached their goals. Other people had more of that adrenalin rush, the excitement, the anticipation of not knowing when or how they would reach their goals. If they went back to school to get a degree, would they be able to finish it? If they applied for a job and got it, would they be able to handle the job? If they started their own business, would they be able to pay their bills and put food on the table? If they committed to a relationship or changed a relationship, how would their life change? These and numerous other situations are all like those rises on the roller coaster with both the thrills and anticipation, but also the fear of a potential drop. What if I don't get the job, don't finish my degree, my business fails, I can't commit to a relationship or regret my decisions about a relationship? In order to handle the rises and the drops, we have to have a positive attitude about unknown outcomes.

Wright

So what you are saying is that by having a positive attitude, life will be great?

Northup

If it were only that easy. I do believe that attitude, whether it is positive or negative, is the basis of every action or outcome we have in our life. And our attitude is formed by our values.

Wright

You mentioned values; how would you define values?

Northup

Values are our deepest beliefs—those things we hold dear and those things we care about the most. Values are what motivate us in our every action and they drive every decision we make. Our values really do influence us and are the basis of the attitudes we have toward self, others, and events in our life.

It really comes down to looking at that first secret of taming life's roller coaster, which is having an awareness of those things that are important to you and those things that happen to you that don't seem to match what you believe in.

David, if I believe that you are an incredible manager—you're the best boss I ever worked for—and then something happens that causes me to question that belief, I have recognized an incongruency. The first secret is having an awareness of what is incongruent. Simply put, incongruence is something that gives you a jolt—something just doesn't seem right. Whether it's a gut feeling, intuition, or insight you have about a situation, it just doesn't fit with who you think you are or what you expected from an interaction or choice you made.

The first secret, *Awareness* is exploring our childhood, our family values, expectations based on our family's beliefs, culture, and our gender. What were the expectations for us growing up? What expectations were self-imposed? When we have awareness and understanding of our values and what drives our decisions and attitudes, then we can move into the second secret, which is, *Perspective*.

Wright

Will you give us more about perspective, the second secret?

Northup

Perspective is really how you interpret events you've had in your life. We can find two people who've had the same situation happen to them. One person will see that situation as negative and crippling and will hold negative thoughts about that situation throughout his or her entire life. That person makes decisions based on the negative impact of that situation. And yet we can find another person who has had the same experience but who will have a totally different perspective. That person reflected on a particular event or relationship and has learned about his or her own emotions and reactions during the event or relationship and has taken the lessons learned and used this positive perspective as a tool to counteract future negative experiences.

So in review, we must have an *awareness* of our deepest beliefs and what experiences are congruent or incongruent with those beliefs. We then must develop a positive *perspective* on past events in our lives.

We've tapped into the first two secrets of taming life's roller coaster and now can move to a stronger *Sense of Self,*—the third secret.

Wright

Don't we all have a strong sense of who we are?

Northup

Most do and yet many people do not have a strong sense of who they are or what they can accomplish. Two people faced with the same situation may respond differently. For example, both are given a new or challenging project. One will say, "Why did they ask me to do that? I haven't had any experience in that. Well, how can I get that done with all the other work I have to do?" In other words, that person's sense of self includes almost a defeatist attitude. And then another person, operating from a strong *Sense of Self,* will say "Fantastic! I get to do something I've always wanted to do. I'm going to show them I really can do this!" That person will see it as a chance of really changing something and say, "Oh good, I have a project where I can do things the way I want to." In other words, the person has an internal strength that says, "I can meet adversity; I can meet change; I can take on challenges and I have the tools [knowledge, characteristics, traits] to make things happen."

Wright

In your fourth secret, *Resolution to Action,* you include goal-setting. Goal-setting isn't really a new idea for getting what you want out of life or taking action.

Northup

You are right, David. Goal-setting is not a new idea but it is critical if we are to be in control of life's *ride.* Most of us are proactive. We have goals, whether they are consciously driven, more subtle, or even subconscious. Others are reactive and shape their lives based on other peoples' decisions, expectations, and goals.

In the fourth secret, Resolution to Action, notice the word "action." We have to move beyond just setting goals and start making decisions and taking the necessary steps to see those goals become a reality. We begin by mapping the steps to change. When we consciously start taking action, we are embracing whatever needs to change in our life to reach our goals. If we set goals without planning a step-by-step approach to get to that goal, we are not embracing the change. We may be embracing the idea of change, but it's only when we take action that we can transform or transition away from a situation that we're in or that we don't want and move toward doing or becoming what we really want as an end result of goal-setting.

Wright

Making a decision to do or not do something isn't always that easy. How do you know the decision you make is the right one?

Northup

You don't—unless you have a crystal ball, and I haven't found one yet! When you decide to take action, there are times when you are making that decision by a leap of faith. That means you move forward trusting that everything will work out and work out the way you expected it to. Other times, making decisions may come from a fear of failure. You don't want to fail so you take the actions to insure that you don't.

Many people fear success more than they fear failure. What they are doing in their goal-setting is thinking about success, but when they start to move toward it, the fear of the unknown may sabotage the actions that are needed to reach that goal.

To counteract any sabotage and become proactive in getting what you want, go back to the first secrets of resilience. Have an awareness of your strongest beliefs (values), look at the ups and downs you have in your life, understand what experiences were congruent or incongruent, and gain a *Perspective* of lessons learned. You now have the strong *Sense of Self* necessary to identify the steps you must take to reach your goal. That's were most of us stop; but we cannot stop here. There must be action motivated by the final step (secret) *Payoff.*

Wright

Payoff is actually a secret—a step that we take?

Northup

That's interesting. I'm asked that frequently. "How can *payoff* actually be a secret?" As we gain *awareness* and *perspective*, develop a strong *sense of self,* and stay true to that sense of self as we take actions, we project ahead to what we will gain when we reach our goals. We look at the payoffs—the positive outcomes. Envisioning positive outcomes is an energizer and strengthens our resolve to get what we want out of life. The more we focus on the payoffs, the easier it is to give our attention to and take the actions that move us toward goal achievement.

Wright

Do you think we have to have a big drop in life before we need to use resilience?

Northup

Absolutely not. Once again, if we go to the image of the roller coaster, the roller coaster isn't just a series of high rises and incredible drops. Sometimes there are smaller rises with smaller drops. Sometimes there are loops on a roller coaster. If you think about some of the rides you have seen at amusement parks, riders are literally "thrown for a loop," as the saying goes. Sometimes there are also small twists, turns, and curves on the roller coaster.

I believe that image is true of life. There are times when we have small ups and downs, incredible ups and downs, and sometimes we are just thrown for a loop. Other times we have twists, turns, and curves but we stay on track. We don't have to hit rock bottom, but the awareness of what ups and downs, twists, turns, curves, and loops may be ahead of us will build our resilience. We have the tools to bounce back and move to a different level of success.

Wright

Are the secrets just for personal use or could companies and organizations use these secrets to improve?

Northup

To answer that let me give you some history on what I discovered when I was working on the idea of resilience. I researched resilience for about two years and could find nothing that revealed much about resilience other than we needed it. I wanted to write about it and couldn't find the data, if you will, to back it up. That's when I started talking to people, and because I am a management consultant, I started talking with my clients about resilience. They initially shared personal examples but quickly went into ways that the organization had drawn on resilience to deal with challenges.

The corporate world has changed, and as we mentioned earlier, has changed quickly. The media bombards us with stories of organizations that are downsizing, companies that are merging, lack of qualified employees, corruption within corporate leadership, and other stories that leave us questioning the stability of our jobs and careers. A perfect example is the plight of the airlines. How many airlines over the past few years have merged with other carriers, filed bankruptcy, received government bailout, or even closed their doors?

As we look at organizations, we find that healthy organizations understand that they have to have in place a way to manage the change, transition, or innovation that's going on in their particular company or industry. In order to prepare for future events, companies must have a resilient workforce. Organizations are investing in resilience training for their employees so that the individuals understand their personal responses to the current or impending changes. Understanding individual and collective resilience of employees assists leadership as they prepare for or implement change.

In summarizing, we find that successful organizations are interested in helping their workforce develop resilience.

Wright

How can organizations know if their employees have resilience?

Northup

The first step would be to monitor the implementation of change. One of the most perfect examples is how quickly our software and hardware need upgrading. We buy a computer and within a few months, we find that it's out of date—there is a better computer or a better software program out there. In the example of changing software and hardware, if we observe that employees are resistant to change, if they refuse to change, or if they justify why they don't need to change, then we can assume that they have questions about the payoff or the outcome of the change. It also says something about their ability to be resilient and the speed at which they could draw upon their resilience.

Wright

In closing, what sets the resilient apart from those who don't have resilience or lose their resilience?

Northup

I would say that those who are resilient have a clear understanding of who they are. They know themselves. They understand where they came from, so to speak. They understand the struggles that they've had. They understand the successes they have had and they have a well defined set of goals and are focused on the payoffs. They are proactive in taking some action every day that moves them closer to a positive future.

About the Author

Dr. Jan Northup is an internationally known author, speaker, organizational strategist, and training specialist. With a degree in education, she has almost thirty years experience in teaching and training development. For the past twenty-five years, Jan has focused her efforts on working with public and private organizations in the areas of employee performance management. As a Professional Behavioral and Values Analyst, she has assisted organizations in meeting all aspects of talent management and employee development through customized training programs and individual and group coaching.

At the same time, she has kept her ties with academia by developing and teaching undergraduate and graduate courses in the areas of organizational design, team building, leadership, and marketing. An on-line course developer, instructor, and adjunct faculty member at Bellevue University, Jan has taught at numerous universities including Thunderbird, The American Graduate School of International Management, and George Washington University.

Advanced training in non-confrontational verbal skills facilitation was such an invaluable tool in working with group dynamics and problem-solving that it led Dr. Northup to develop the S.P.A.C.E. (Superior Performance and Communications Excellence) training program which has been given in private and government environments.

Dr. Northup created "The Promotable Woman: What Makes the Difference" video training program that has been featured on the Public Broadcasting Service. She has made frequent radio and television appearances, discussing the factors that make the difference in the lives of successful people. Close to a million people worldwide have attended her seminars, training classes, and presentations. She has been a featured speaker at numerous regional and national conferences and was the first woman to conduct a nationwide speaking tour of Australia on women's management issues. In recognition of her professional and community accomplishments, she has been the recipient of numerous awards and commendations. She is a member of the Phoenix Chamber of Commerce facilitating the Professional Women's Roundtable, a life-time member of the American Association of University Women, and has served on the Board of Directors for Girls Ranch Inc. of Arizona. Dr. Northup's latest books, *Life's a Bitch and Then You Change Your Attitude: 5 Secrets to Taming Life's Roller Coaster and Building Resilience,* examines personal and organizational resilience; *Speaking of Success* with Ken Blanchard, Stephen Covey, Jack Canfield, and other leading authors (a compilation of success strategies); and *The Promotable Woman: Have We Come A Long Way Baby?* updates earlier research on women in the workplace.

Dr. Jan Northup
Management Training Systems, Inc.
P.O. Box 11806
Glendale, AZ 85318
Phone: 623.587.7644
E-mail: jnkmts@msn.com
www.trainingperformance.com
www.thebizcoach4u.com

Chapter 5

DAVID FRANKLIN FARKAS

THE INTERVIEW

David Wright (Wright)
I am talking with David Franklin Farkas of HouseHealing.com. David, welcome to *Rising to the Top: A Guide to Success.*

David Farkas (Farkas)
Thank you.

Wright
David, you have an unusual business . . . tell us about it.

Farkas
You're right. House healing and "ghost-busting" are not everyday, run-of-the-mill businesses. Because of that, I get a broad range of reactions. There are some people who are immediately fascinated and excited and there are others who raise their eyebrows or who are put off by it. The response is all over the place.

Wright

Who would use your services?

Farkas

The two main groups that would use my services are people involved in real estate transactions or people who, because they are already familiar with an alternative approach to healing in their lives, realize that the place they are living may not be perfect for them and they want to improve the "energy" of the place.

The mainstays of my business are situations where a piece of real estate is mysteriously not selling. Based on all the normally addressed characteristics of the property and the market place, it looks like it should be selling, but it just won't sell. Sometimes the property does not even get showings.

A common story I hear from realtors all the time is that people walk into a house and say, "This is a great place, but I just don't know what it is . . . there is just something that isn't quit right for me." Then they complain about the size of the windows or whether there is a marble countertop. They make something up that lets them rationalize their feeling. They are feeling something in their body that they cannot define and they don't have any skills to understand or discern. But, they know that something isn't quite right.

That "something that isn't quite right" is my specialty.

Wright

That's fascinating. You can really affect all that? This is pretty strange stuff.

Farkas

Well, I have a good track record.

Let me give you an example. One particular house had been on the market a while and there was a negotiation in process, but it was not closing. Three days after I worked on the house they had a deal.

But, while what I do is effective, the things I can affect are an open system and a very dynamic system. There are lots of things affecting everything that goes on any place and often the emotions of the people involved will affect whether or not a house will sell. That is something that I can deal with as well.

Wright

What do you mean?

Farkas

I tune into and modify the energy of a building and that affects the way the property feels, which affects whether it sells and also affects the people who live and work in that building. But, let's back up and create a context for what I do.

Both quantum physics and all the mystical traditions tell us that everything is energy. Science began to understand this from Einstein's early experiments with light. Until his work, science always thought of light as being electromagnetic waves, which of course, it is. But Einstein realized something else was going on. One of his early papers say that, "It looks, in the math, like light may be *lumpy.*" It isn't just a wave. From that came the idea that light is both a wave and a stream of particles called photons.

Everything in our universe is both an electromagnetic wave with frequency and information and particles—solid matter. The reverse is also true: what seems to be solid is also an electromagnetic wave.

What is even more fascinating is that the experiments show that those particles only appear when we look for them. In some way our observation creates a particle out of the wave. Our choice—what we focus on—takes all the possible outcomes and crystallizes it into a solid form. Physicists call that "collapsing the wave form."

It is really fascinating stuff. There are even experiments that show that a particle can be in two places at the same time. It is not that there are two particles and they interact, but that one particle can be in more than one place.

So, the way I look at my work is that everything is energy, everything is connected, and everything is interactive. Mystics all over the planet have said this for thousands of years. Physics is now proving it.

One mystery of quantum physics is that when you observe a particle in an experiment it behaves differently than if it is not being observed. Is this because there is an interaction between the scientist who is the observer and the experiment itself?

Scientists—physicists—will tell you that when they are doing an experiment they limit the number of variables and they stay out of the experimental results. I am as much of a scientist as they are, but I know I am the scientist, the observer, and the lab equipment.

Now there is no lab equipment that will tune into what I tune into, yet. It appears that the frequencies that describe what I do are much higher than anything that is presently measured. But, there are many people all over the world who can tune into those frequencies.

At some point there will be equipment that can do it, but right now there isn't.

I tune into and modify the energy of a building and that affects the way the property feels, which affects whether it sells and also affects the people who live and work in that building.

So my work is a practical application of these concepts in quantum physics. I interact with the energy of the building or the person to get the desired outcome in physical reality.

Wright

So, David, you mentioned that houses can be traumatized?

Farkas

When I look at a building in the meditative state, I enter to do my work and I will see a network of lines—a grid. It looks almost like graph paper made out of light. But, instead of the geometry that consists of continuous straight lines that cross correctly, there are usually ragged holes in the grid as if it had shattered.

What I have discovered is that those holes appear to have been created by human emotions, by major dramas, or major traumas. They literally have enough physical forces to damage the underlying energy structure. In addition to that, what I have found totally fascinating is that the story—the actual emotions and story of that trauma—become stored in the hole. Everyone who comes into that building is affected by this background story that is still running in the building. It also appears that the people who buy or live in a particular house must have some kind of resonance with those earlier traumas. There will be something in their family history or something that is similar to that story in their own life story or they couldn't live there.

So, when people go into a house and say, "I don't know what it is, but this isn't right," they are saying that whatever drama occurred there is not something that resonates for them. When people walk into a building and say, "This feels great," they have a resonance with what has happened there and the house is comfortable for them.

One aspect of my work is our proprietary *Quantum Grid Restructuring* protocol. Its affect is much like reformatting a computer's hard drive. When you reformat a hard drive it is still usable, but the old files are gone and you can now put your files into it. In the case of houses and buildings, the new "files" are the emotions and dramas of the new owners or tenants.

This level of clearing is a service that I provide that I have not found anyone else doing.

Wright

So you look at things differently than a scientist would?

Farkas

Well, I think that sometime in the future, when the technology is available to work at very high electromagnetic frequencies, scientists will come up with ways of observing and confirming these phenomena.

Parapsychologists study energetic phenomena and things like ghosts by getting photographs and audio imprints. They work to confirm that ghosts are real.

I just talk to the ghosts. Because I can do that, I can assist in the rescue of these lost souls and that too makes a building feel very different.

Wright

You call yourself a real estate consultant. How can you help realtors or people buying and selling property?

Farkas

Well, every transaction has its little traumas and in my experience many of those problems that crop up have to do with issues that are on other levels, whether it is historical dramas or something like a ghost in the house.

From my perspective, if realtors or brokers were working with me on a consistent basis their transactions would go through more quickly. People would look at their results and wonder, "Why are you selling properties that I can't sell?"

Every realtor has inventory they can't sell or at least won't sell at market value. If the realtor was to work with me, things would go more smoothly and he or she would make more money.

Typically I get business when somebody is having a problem with a real estate sale and they are looking for a solution. They find me through word-of-mouth or through some marketing piece I have out there. But as this work becomes better known I think there are going to be more realtors who realize, "This service is just a nominal charge for something that is going to grease the wheels of my business, so I am just going to have this done on every property." We are happy to have retainer arrangements with clients who work with us on an ongoing basis.

Wright

What are the legal issues?

Farkas

As far as I know there are none. My work does not involve any apparent interaction in the physical world.

The clients have an issue and I do something. This is true for most consultants. You never know what they are doing. They talk to you, get some information, and go back to their office. They could be beating a drum and chanting for all you know. Then they come back with suggestions and if what they suggest works more than half the time you are more than happy to pay them. They know things that you don't know.

In a really basic way, that is my business. You give me information, I do what I do, and a substantial portion of the time the outcome is an improvement in your situation.

I am a consultant like any other consultant; the difference is that I talk about the strange things I do and a lot of consultants don't. I am essentially like any other consultant applying my knowledge and spending time focusing on your problem in the hope that the knowledge and skills I have will move the business transaction forward, and my track record is good.

Wright

What is "Stigmatized Property"?

Farkas

Well, Stigmatized Property is one of those strange, dirty little secrets or perhaps the skeleton in the closet of the real estate business. Many properties have had a crime committed in them and that may include violence, murder, suicide or someone died in the house from some other cause. Many properties have a reputation of being haunted—there is just something strange going on there.

As soon as the house gets that kind of reputation people tend not to want to buy it. And this is even true of people who will vehemently tell you they don't believe in ghosts or "bad vibes."

There are all kinds of legal implications. In some jurisdictions realtors have to give information to the buyer. There are some jurisdictions that require disclosure if there has been a murder in the last three years on the property or in the house/building. In some places only suicides need to be disclosed. In other jurisdictions, if you disclose the information, you are legally liable because you have now given information that affects the value of the house.

It is complicated legally, but it is not complicated in terms of my business. In situations where the house is not selling and it is a "stigmatized property," I have, in several instances, been able to see what is going on that makes the place feel strange and I can do a remediation. Then the house feels different and people are more willing to purchase it in spite of the property's reputation.

Perhaps at some point in the future I will be able to develop some kind of certification that says I have looked at the property and indeed it was haunted and I have "chased the ghosts off." I actually don't chase them off—this work is about rescuing them. Ghosts are lost, confused, and stuck.

Whether this process would ever be something that the legal system and the realty industry would accept, I don't know. What I do know is that under these circumstances, after I work on a house, the house typically sells because it feels different after those issues have been dealt with.

Wright

It seems that most people don't know anything about what you do. Aren't most people afraid to be in a place that has a ghost?

Farkas

Sure. Most people are, for a lack of a better term, "spooked" by ghosts because they don't know anything about them. All they know is that under certain circumstances they see or hear something for a fleeting moment or feel a chill up their back. That scares them because they don't know what it is. Like anything else in life, once you find out what is going on and how it works, it is not scary anymore.

One of my talks is called *Everything You Know about Ghosts is Dead Wrong.* That program is really a debunking process because most people are getting their information from the popular media. If you have watched movies like *Poltergeist* and the *Omen* (which, by the way I have never watched because they are creepy, scary movies) the information you have taken in is wrong. They are showing phenomena that have nothing to do with ghosts and are saying that a ghost caused it. A lot of movies get it wrong and a lot of information from other sources is wrong.

Like everything else in the world, ghosts are just phenomena; there is a way to understand what happens when somebody dies and why certain spirits or souls don't move on to where they would normally go after death. What is that about? How does it happen? How and why do they interact with you? What is going on here?

Since I do this stuff everyday, it is pretty matter-of-fact to me and I can explain it to people. Usually after understanding the phenomenon people say "oh, my goodness, that is all that is going on here." It takes all that mystery out of it and it gives them skills.

I call it "six secrets everyone should know" because the word "secret" just means knowledge that most people don't have. After you get the six secrets and you have an understanding of ghosts, I can share a couple of things that anyone can do when interacting with ghost. Then these situations are not as creepy anymore.

Wright

What an interesting conversation. I really appreciate your giving our readers a better understanding of what it is that you do.

Farkas

Thank you.

About the Author

DAVID FRANKLIN FARKAS, consultant, intuitive and spiritual healer, specializes in remote energetic and spiritual clearing of buildings, places, people, and businesses. He works with individuals and organizations to help them remove unseen blocks and obstacles that have kept them from moving forward to the achievement of their goals.

David is also a lively, funny, and effective speaker and trainer and is available in person or by teleseminar.

His popular signature presentation is "Everything You Know About Ghosts is Dead Wrong." He also talks about "Stigmatized Real Estate" and about the secrets behind "The Secret" including his workshop, "Is Free Will Really Free?"

David Franklin Farkas
Phone: 888-5-RUBICON
E-mail: realty@farkas.com
www.Farkas.com

Chapter 6

SHARON WINGRON, CPLP

THE INTERVIEW

David Wright (Wright)

Today we're talking with Sharon Wingron, CPLP. Sharon has proven her success as a leader in the workplace learning and performance field by being one of the first two hundred and fifty people ever to earn the prestigious ASTD Certified Professional in Learning and Performance (CPLP) designation, serving on the 2007–2008 ASTD Board of Directors and as chair of the National Advisors for Chapters, becoming St. Louis' first certified DiSC® trainer, and consistently producing as a top 1 percent authorized distributor of Inscape Publishing products. Her success is built on significant staff, line, and consulting experience in diverse industries spanning eighteen countries across North America, Europe, Africa, and Asia. With more than twenty years of experience in training, organizational development, management and leadership development, first line supervision, process improvement, and business operations, she has helped thousands of people be the best that they can be, reach their goals, and increase their ability to influence and lead others. Sharon has an MBA from Southern Illinois University–Edwardsville, and a BS in

Engineering Management with a Psychology minor from the Missouri University of Science and Technology (formally known as University of Missouri–Rolla).

Sharon, welcome to *Rising to the Top: A Guide to Success*.

Sharon Wingron (Wingron)

Thanks, David, I'm glad to be here.

Wright

The name of your business is Wings of Success LLC. That seems to make you a natural fit for this book! Let's start with asking the obvious question. How do you define success?

Wingron

David, I've contemplated that quite a bit through the years, especially as I considered the name for my business, the contribution I wanted to make, and the reputation I wanted to develop. How would the services and products I offer act as "Wings" of Success?

For me, success relates to a quote by Ralph Waldo Emerson that begins, "To laugh often and much, to win the respect of intelligent people, and affection of children . . ." then it continues with several thoughts, finally ending with, ". . . to know even one life has breathed easier because you have lived. This is to have succeeded." To me, that quote summarizes success; it's something that I believe is personally defined.

It is limiting to define success by external factors such as how much money you've made or if you have a business card and what the title on it is. I believe that each person must define what success will look like in his or her own life. People should decide for themselves what the goals are that excite them and what would be most meaningful to them. And ultimately, they should decide what contributions they really want to make to the world. Who do they want to be and how do they want to live their lives?

I believe when a person is intentional in life—creating the life they choose, living it on purpose, and achieving the goals they've set for themselves—that's when they have succeeded.

Wright

Interesting—it's not about material success, but about personal success. Our book is titled *Rising to the Top: A Guide to Success*. What do you think it takes to get to the top?

Wingron

Well, David, going back to the definition of success we've discussed, the first thing people need to figure out is what "the top"
means to them. What are they trying to get to the top of? For example, do they want to become professionally recognized? Do they want
to make a significant positive contribution, regardless of whether or
not they are recognized or paid for it? Is it monetary wealth or social
status they are seeking? Or is it simply that they want to be the best
parent, friend, or person they can possibly be? I really think the top
could be anything, depending on who you are, your values, and aspirations.

In the book *Good to Great*, researcher and author, Jim Collins,
discusses what he calls the "Hedgehog Concept." Imagine a Venn dia-
gram with three overlapping circles. Each circle represents a key decision. The first is what you can be best in the world at (you define
your world). The second is what you are deeply passionate about. The
third circle represents what drives your economic engine or, put
another way, what people will pay you to do. The intersection of these
three circles—where they overlap—represents the Hedgehog Concept.

Collins and his research team did a comparative study of companies that were "good" performers with companies that rose and became great performers given similar opportunities, challenges, and
economic environments. He found that one of the key distinguishing
factors was that the great performers identified their unique Hedgehog Concept and focused on it with steadfast commitment.

I believe individuals can use that same model to determine their
focus area and what their "top" could be. What are they so passionate
about and talented at that they would do it even if nobody paid them?
But people *will* want to pay them for it, so it can sustain them physically as well as mentally, emotionally, and spiritually.

Rising to the top takes focus, so when you can find that "sweet
spot" that brings you joy and provides your livelihood, you are less
likely to get distracted by the business and maintenance of life, and
you can focus on giving your best—that is what the Hedgehog Concept offers.

I think once people know what it is that they are striving for—
what the "top" is for them—then a few more key things will help
them get there.

First, if people want to rise to the top they need to make the decision to be a leader. To me, that means focusing on serving others,
owning the consequences of your choices, and performing acts of lea-

dership. Not being a leader from the standpoint of power or glory or authority, but really serving others and helping them—knowing that you're not rising to the top through ambition, but through service.

The second is to know yourself deeply—cultivating your ability to be authentic and true to yourself. Developing what is known as *emotional intelligence* is a key aspect of this. There are four main components to emotional intelligence: self-awareness, self-management, interpersonal awareness, and relationship management. Rising to the top requires you to "do your work"—acknowledge your strengths and limitations, let go of your fears and inhibitions, take risks to overcome your challenges, and stretch yourself.

Last, you must direct your intentions and actions toward becoming the best that you can personally be. This involves a lifelong commitment to continuous learning and continuous improvement.

Wright

Continuous learning and improvement—I can see how that is crucial for people to rise to the top. That makes me think of forward motion. Sharon, the word "Wings" in your business name evokes images of people soaring to success. What qualifies you to help people soar?

Wingron

Great question David! As I mentioned before, I thought about that a lot when I started my business over five years ago. I'm a big fan of John Maxwell and Stephen Covey and the work that they've done on leadership.

One of the things they talk about is that people need to have a combination of character and competence. I'd like to think that this is what I offer to people, so they trust me enough to let me help them become successful. I love people (my license plate even spells out the word "PEOPLE") and I really believe in them! My personal mission statement can be summarized as: "Love, Share Joy, Discover, Learn, Teach." This involves my quest to have a positive impact on every person I meet. The fact that I care about people and want to help them shows up in my actions. People sense my enthusiasm and integrity around this.

On the character side, I have an ongoing commitment to continuous improvement and honesty about the fact that I'm "doing my own work" and continuing to improve myself and my situation. A guiding principle I follow in my business is that I will only teach or consult on that which I am actively trying to live. This transparency and authenticity really resonates with people; it allows them to open up and be vulnerable with me while equipping me to be someone who can serve them and help them reach their goals. People see I am real—not a slick expert who has all the answers, but instead, a down-to-earth person who is also on a learning journey. They realize I can share insights and experience, ask questions, and hold them account-able in a way that spurs growth and achievement because I am "walking in their shoes" at the same time.

On the competency side (a bit of a more tangible level to some), I think what qualifies me is that I've led a blessed life filled with a great combination of business and workplace learning and perfor-mance experience and credentials. I'm one of the few people who have a technical (engineering) degree coupled with an MBA and an under-standing of psychology and people. With a business and manufactur-ing background, I've had the opportunity to work across many func-tional areas—customer service, production, engineering, organization development, and human resources. This helps me to see the systems perspective, speak many organizational languages, and really under-stand the challenges and opportunities of the line leaders and staff I work with.

Wright

I would hire you Sharon—you certainly seem to have both charac-ter and competence!

Some research suggests that the "hard" moments or challenging experiences in life have the greatest developmental impact on a per-son. What are some of these "defining moments" that have contri-buted to your success?

Wingron

I like to think of the tough experiences as "slam dancing with real-ity" because sometimes you get into things and you're just banging your way through trying to figure it out!

One of the really crucial learning experiences I had was the time I spent as a first line supervisor of teamsters in a brewery. They were all men; I was the first woman supervisor on the brewing side of the plant, and I was at least ten years younger than the workforce I ma-naged. Needless to say, that was a character-building experience! Everything I thought I knew about how to be a manager and how to work with people, to a large extent got turned upside down because it was such a challenging environment; it seemed to me that "how it works" didn't always work there.

As I struggled with the environment and my role, I went through a period of time when I was extremely discouraged and depressed. When enough people had told me that I wasn't being myself—my natural enthusiasm and optimism were seriously waning—I decided to seek help through the company's employee assistance program and get counseling. I found the process of reaching out to get help and getting a different perspective on what I was going through was extremely useful for me. The counselor helped me remember my strengths, look at the situation differently, and explore options. Ultimately what I found was "empowerment."

One definition of empowerment that really resonates with me is "to release the power within." When I was going through this experience struggling as a supervisor, I heard that definition. What I learned was that I really wasn't releasing my own power, so to speak. I was letting the situation and the challenging interactions with people bring me down instead of tapping into my own strengths, my own character, and my *authentic* power. It was a defining moment for me. I realized that it was up to *me* to make choices about how I interacted in the world, about how happy I was, about what kind of life experience I was having and would have in the future.

I decided I would never let anyone take that power away from me again. From that point on I got very purposeful about where I was taking my life, the decisions I was making, and how I wanted to "show up" as a person.

Wright

It's obvious that you are passionate about people being empowered and holding themselves accountable. Why is that so important to you?

Wingron

I've felt the difference it makes first-hand. Life is so much richer and more rewarding when you release your own power to make a positive contribution to the world.

People often seem to have a "victim" mentality. They feel like they are trapped by a situation they are in—the "golden handcuffs," their managers "making" them feel horrible—but really, they are just giving away their own power and they don't even realize that they are choosing to stay in these negative situations.

I want to help people realize that life is all about the choices they make. It really is about how you are choosing to respond to the situation you are in, the choices you made that led you to any given point in time and circumstance, what steps you want to take to move on, or what steps you want to take to come to peace with whatever situation you are in.

Perhaps most powerfully, people need to realize that regardless of where they are now, they can choose where they are going next. As we discussed earlier regarding success, when we direct our intentions and actions toward a desired outcome, amazing things can happen! It is all about releasing our authentic God-given power. When people feel empowered and hold themselves accountable for their success or failure in life, I think it makes all the difference in the world.

Wright

What do you think are the biggest obstacles people face in releasing their power and achieving success?

Wingron

From what I've seen, emotional intelligence is a key factor. Daniel Goleman and many others have done much work to bring this topic to the forefront of current thinking.

Remember the four "buckets" of emotional intelligence I referenced earlier: self-awareness, self-management, interpersonal awareness, and relationship management. Just like so many things in life, awareness is the first step! The father of leadership, Peter Drucker, noted, "Reflection is one of the most overlooked leadership tools."

One obstacle is that people get too busy in life just going through their daily activities and they don't take time to reflect and get to know themselves better. They might brush things off as "just the way I am" and not recognize the habits they have cultivated and the impact their behaviors are having on the people around them and the results they are getting. They might get into a conflict with someone or get upset about something, but not notice this is as part of a pattern that has developed in their life. They might get through the moment, but not take the time to analyze and break the pattern. They then wonder "why do these things always happen to me?"

A related obstacle is that people often aren't aware of what their strengths, challenge areas, or limitations are. Moving to self-management, once they are aware they either write it off or they put blame on others. They don't take time to recognize that once they know their strengths they can capitalize on them.

The Gallup Organization continues to demonstrate through their research that people who focus on their strengths tend to be the most successful, yet so many people focus instead on their weaknesses. They try to become someone they aren't instead of owning their strengths, building on them, as well as owning their limitations and learning to manage that behavior or putting systems in place to minimize the negative impact of those limitations.

People often see others as "the problem." Another obstacle is that we focus on changing others instead of working on ourselves. We have to start with managing ourselves better, then we can work on understanding others better and adapting to work more effectively with them. Many people just aren't paying the price to get to know themselves and to figure out how they can first make those choices and take those actions to be the best they can be. They try to change others as opposed to becoming a role model that others will want to follow. This reminds me of the Gandhi quote, "Be the change you want to see in the world."

Wright

Sounds like emotional intelligence is a crucial foundation for becoming successful. How do you help people develop emotional intelligence, thus setting them up for success?

Wingron

In my work I offer a variety of seminars, workshops, consulting, and coaching as well as delivering keynote speeches. All of these services focus on raising my clients' self-awareness and self-management as a foundation. This is the beginning of what I call "Personal Excellence." Depending on the engagement, we also move in to the more advanced areas of interpersonal awareness and relationship management. These areas are crucial for "Organizational Performance" and "Leadership Effectiveness."

I frequently use self-assessment instruments and designed learning processes to help people develop emotional intelligence. I find that when people do a self-assessment, they perceive the information as more meaningful because it is objective data based on research and statistical validation. They learn about themselves in a way that feels more actionable and less threatening as opposed to taking it personally as one might when someone he or she knows provides direct feedback. It takes behavior out of the subjective nature of perception (i.e., "So and so thinks you're this or that") and enables people to understand that there are some predictable human behaviors. They can learn about themselves and others and learn strategies for becoming more effective.

Two of the assessment tools I do a lot of work with are the DiSC® Behavioral Styles profile and BRAIN MODE® *power* for Professional Development. The DiSC® model provides nonjudgmental language for exploring behavioral issues across four primary dimensions. Each style has its own strengths and limitations:

"D" is for the "dominance" behavioral style. People with a D style have a need for accomplishment and getting things done. They are direct and decisive. Sometimes they come across a bit like control freaks to others, and yet they are really just trying to move projects forward.

People with an I or "influence," style have a need for social recognition and influence. They tend to be optimistic and outgoing. They can sometimes get themselves over-committed and that can cause problems for themselves or for others, yet the enthusiasm and excitement they bring to projects really keeps people engaged.

People with the S or "steadiness" style have a need for acceptance and stability. They tend to be sympathetic and cooperative. They are often good process people, and really work to keep harmony in teams. Sometimes they struggle with being able to make changes quickly or to effectively deal with conflict.

Finally the people with the C or "conscientiousness" style have a need for analysis and correctness. They tend to be our data people who are so crucial for making right decisions. If they're not careful, however, they can get hung up on taking too much time to analyze, and people can perceive them as in "analysis paralysis."

Wright

I'm thinking of people I know already, just from those brief descriptions! I can also see myself in there. I can see how this tool could be effective in helping people understand themselves and others better. Understanding people certainly is important to success.

Wingron

Yes! DiSC® is an excellent tool, and it provides a powerful foundation for building emotional intelligence because it really starts with helping people become more aware of what their own tendencies are, their motivations, their fears, limitations, and it helps them realize some of these behaviors are predictable. They come to realize it's not so scary and it's not "just me." Instead, they realize "wow, there's a group of people like me out there!" Our society typically focuses on our weaknesses and often people aren't proud of who they are and what they naturally bring to the table. One reason DiSC® is so powerful is because it helps people accept and honor their strengths. This goes back to "releasing the power within" that we discussed earlier. My clients learn to build on their strengths effectively, manage their challenge areas, and manage those perceptions others may have about them. This is very empowering for them.

The other assessment tool I mentioned, BRAIN MODE®*power*, is a newer tool on the market. It's a tool to help people understand their learning and thinking styles. There's a very simple online self-assessment that enables people to learn how they learn! Do they tend to learn more through being auditory, visual, or kinesthetic? "Kinesthetic" means that they need to be actively involved with things—moving and manipulating their bodies—to engage in learning. The assessment also identifies people's thinking styles—do they think more globally, sequentially, or with a more integrated approach?

Knowing your learning and thinking style is interesting, but the power of the BRAIN MODE®*power* toolset is in the very practical, easy-to-apply strategies for putting that knowledge into action, which is included in the report as well as in a follow-on series of "Brain-Builder" messages that participants receive. For example, I realize that I'm an extremely global and visual person, so I put that information to action in how I organized my working space. I created a "project room" with a big white board on one entire wall so that I can *think big* and *see what I'm thinking* to help me process through projects and challenges I'm facing.

It's a great tool for any learning situation or for any person who wants to use his or her brain more effectively. The tool also helps you learn to identify others' learning and thinking styles so you can communicate more effectively with them.

Again, we start with self-awareness and self-management, and then move into interpersonal awareness and relationship management. This is a proven approach for setting people up for success.

Wright

On your Web site, www.developPEOPLE.com, you emphasize that you work with individuals and teams to "develop PEOPLE™"

(PEOPLE is a trademarked acronym for "Personal Excellence—Organizational Performance—Leadership Effectiveness"). How does developing these qualities help people become successful?

Wingron
Well, David, it all begins with Personal Excellence, knowing yourself, and releasing your own power as a positive contribution to the world. How do you define what success means to you? How do you define what's your top? Once you know who you are and what you're about, how can you *really become the best possible you* that you can be? I believe that is the foundation of success—getting clear on who you are, what your strengths are, what contribution you can make, and executing on that to your fullest capability.

The next two really feed together. I strongly believe in the importance of leadership at a personal and professional level. I don't look at leadership as tied to a position in an organization or being about the level of authority you have. I think it's about who you *choose* to be. How do you lead your own life? Are you trustworthy? Then how do you provide leadership to others? Do people trust you? Are you serving your constituents' needs and working toward the larger good? Are you getting the results you are seeking? Are you having a positive influence? If you are, that is "Leadership Effectiveness."

"Organizational Performance" requires this leadership effectiveness at the top of the organization and throughout the organization. Today leaders must develop organizations where each individual is "engaged" in the work—they are committed to excellence, fully involved in and enthusiastic about their work.

The Gallup Organization has been a thought leader researching and writing about the "engagement" factor and the impact it has on organizational performance. Their research shows that the higher percentage of "engaged" workers a company has, the better results that company achieves—productivity, profitability, safety, etc.—all key measures are better. When people are engaged in their work, they're bringing their Personal Excellence to whatever they are doing, and acting as leaders throughout the organization. They are releasing their power!

Great leadership thinkers like Peter Drucker and John Kotter have distinguished management as being about efficiency, and leadership as being about effectiveness. When we combine these—leadership and management—we get excellent leaders tapping into each person's excellence. That is how we get to organizational performance! We put in appropriate systems and processes and establish a culture built on trust and accountability in which each person can perform at his or her peak. This is how organizations can get sustainable positive business results.

Wright

I notice that you emphasize both personal and organizational leadership in the context of discussing success. What does it mean to be a leader?

Wingron

Many people have studied and written about leadership through the years, often with varying perspectives. I think it is important to develop your own "leadership point of view."

First, I think it is important to realize the old myth of "leaders being born, not made" has been completely disproved by current research. While people may be born with certain characteristics like charisma that pre-dispose them to be perceived as a leader, these characteristics do not automatically make a person a leader.

Second, it is important to realize that leadership is situational. Different situations demand different types of leadership. In crises, you may need a "command and control" leader. In a growing company, you may need an empowering leader who builds great teams and instills consistent processes. This is why I refer to performing "acts of leadership." When a person assesses a situation and steps up to exert influence toward accomplishing an outcome in that moment, he or she is acting as a leader.

This is why I believe *leadership is a choice*. It begins with making a choice that you want to be a positive influence on others and you are willing to be held accountable for your decisions and actions. It's about deciding: "How can I best serve my organization and how can I best serve the people I lead? How can I serve collectively to enable us to achieve the organizational goals we are working toward?" "Regardless of what role I'm in, how can I make a positive difference in working to create an environment where people willingly give their best?" Anyone in any job at any level of an organization can be a leader in this way.

I've heard it said that, "Leaders are dealers in hope." As a leader, you must consider, "How can I help people honestly evaluate the situation they are in, and yet help give them hope for the future?" Being able to help others find perspective, assisting them in creating action plans, and supporting them as they take action are all crucial parts of what it means to be a leader. We hear about leaders "casting a vision;" being a dealer in hope is part of that process!

Sometimes people need help in seeing a situation or a life differently from what they are currently experiencing, so being a leader means being a coach at times: helping them think it through, feel understood, giving them new ideas, providing direct feedback about what is working and what isn't, helping them explore ways to remove barriers, and providing resources. Being a leader means always seeking an answer to the question of "how can I make a positive difference for each person I interact with?"

Wright

I've heard you mention the saying "facilitate more than you present" as a key approach for leaders at all levels in an organization. I've only heard that phrase used in regard to training before. Would you tell me more about how you see this as a crucial leadership skill?

Wingron

I found my home in the training and development world after transitioning from manufacturing and engineering, and it really impacted me the first time I heard that phrase "facilitate more than you present." I had always thought the most important skill for being an effective trainer was to have great presentation skills. I learned that while those skills are important to have, they are not the most important—facilitation skills are. There is a related saying in the training world: "Be the guide on the side, not the sage on the stage." As a trainer your job is not to be the expert with all the answers, but instead, your goal should be to help people learn the material. So in essence, you need to be more of a facilitator than a "trainer" or "presenter."

A definition of facilitate that I really like is "to make easy." So when I think of facilitation and "facilitating more than you present" with regard to leadership, it's really about *making easy* whatever the people you are working with or leading are trying to accomplish. You're not "telling" what to do; you're not giving them the answers. You're not trying to be that all-knowing sage, but instead you are taking more of a coaching approach—you help them think through what they are experiencing. You recognize that people often have the answers within themselves so you support them, ask questions, guide them, offer resources, and you break down barriers and resistance.

The more that you develop a relationship built on trust and support, the more you will begin to release that power within, which goes back to empowerment as we discussed before. You *facilitate* the process of their having confidence in themselves, defining their own goals, discovering solutions, and achieving success. You guide your people with their individual goals toward alignment with the organizational goals—whether it's a volunteer organization you're working within or a for-profit organization or even if it's a family. As a leader you want to facilitate—make easy for others—what they are trying to accomplish.

Wright

You facilitate or make easy their success. That's a great perspective for a leader to take, Sharon.

In addition to what we've already discussed, please tell me more about the services and products you offer that help your clients achieve success through developing their PEOPLE.™

Wingron

We provide a variety of services and products through Wings of Success. For the "do-it-yourself-ers," we have the self-assessments and facilitation kits that skilled trainers and facilitators can use within their own organizations to train the people they support and help them develop their PEOPLE™skills. These include products like the DiSC® assessments, Time Mastery, Personal Listening Skills, etc. We have a whole range of tools to help develop emotional intelligence and Personal Effectiveness. These are available both online and in hard copy formats and the facilitation materials can be used out of the box or can be customized. Clients can establish their own electronic profile center where they can personalize and manage the assessments they use, create group reports, and more. This is a very rich resource for organizations that are serious about developing their PEOPLE™and moving the organization to more success.

On a more customized basis we offer executive coaching to assist leaders such as CEOs, presidents, mid- and upper-level managers to become more effective leaders, taking that coaching approach to helping them think about who they are as leaders and how to improve the impact they are having. We help them explore what they are trying to accomplish and how they can best serve their stakeholders.

From a leadership development standpoint, we provide services to develop both individual and organizational leaders. For individuals, we offer an exciting experiential program called "Accountability in Action" during which participants explore the aspects of success and leadership we've been discussing and formulate their plans for turning the learning into action.

For organizational leadership we are an affiliate of The Integró Leadership Institute. Integró utilizes processes that develop cultures of trust and accountability. We have an entire suite of products that help senior teams gain alignment in the organization to make sure that they are all on board with the vision they are working toward, the roles that they play, and how they work together. We have 360 degree assessments we offer through which the leadership teams or other leaders of the organization can get feedback from their peers and direct reports to identify strengths and gaps, then work toward developing key competencies.

We offer "The Team Alignment Questionnaire" that is a tool to assess the level of trust in the organization. Do people trust where the organization is going? Do they trust their leadership team to take them there? Trust is crucial to employee engagement. If employees don't trust the leadership, they are less likely to be engaged in the work and organizational performance suffers.

Finally, we have the longer-term offerings that include the Team Development Process and Leadership Development Process. These encompass "distributed learning" and "reflective learning" over a course of twelve to eighteen months where participants intermittently come together in workshops and work on learning new skills as well as addressing business-specific challenges. The participants are expected to go back and share knowledge with their organizations, while working on developing the skills back on the job before they come to the next workshop. The leaders learn to live the skills and become coaches, teaching the skills to their team members along the way.

Throughout everything we offer at Wings of Success we really believe that learning is a *process* and we want to take a solutions approach. While we can offer our products, we always follow that up with consultation and advisory services to help our clients maximize their use and the results they get from whatever product or service they are using. It is about facilitating our clients' success!

Wright

In summary, what is the most important message you want our readers to take away about success and how they can achieve it?

Wingron

I think the most important message is that this life is really up to us. Success is up to us! First, recognize that you *can* achieve whatever you want to achieve if you draw on your strengths, focus, and channel your energy into working toward the goal. Figure out who you are and what your "Hedgehog Concept" is, then make the choice for success! Determine what the knowledge, skills, and attitudes are that you need to achieve that success—what resources you need to tap into—and then be willing to work for it, continuously gaining experience, learning, and improving.

When we see people on television or read about them in magazines, it is often easy to assume they have been "overnight successes." That is what the media often leads us to believe. But inevitably, if you dig into the background of someone who is considered to be an "overnight success," you find out the many things that person has been doing to become successful. You would find that the individual has been working the odd jobs to make money to pay for school, practicing longer and harder than his or her peers, contacting hundreds of people a day, or whatever else it took over the course of ten or twenty years before the "overnight" success status was achieved! It didn't happen suddenly, it happened because of the person's commitment and the choices made every day.

Ultimately, success is about the choices you make and your efforts to continuously work to learn and improve.

Wright

I appreciate your taking this time to answer all these questions for me. I know I have learned a lot, and I think our readers will as well.

Wingron

Thank you, David; it's been a joy to talk with you! I'm looking forward to hearing what the other experts have said and learning from them also. Here's wishing you success!

The information on behavioral styles is adapted from the widely used DiSC® model and DISC Classic. DISC Classic is copyrighted 2001 by Inscape Publishing, Inc., Minneapolis, Minnesota. "DISC" and "Inscape Publishing" are registered trademarks of

---

About the Author

SHARON WINGRON, President of Wings of Success LLC, a workplace learning and performance (WLP) firm, believes that each person has inherent strengths and dreams waiting to be culled out and developed to make a meaningful contribution in the world. She believes there is power and success in aligning these personal attributes to individual and organizational goals. Sharon's personal mission statement can be summarized as "Love, Share Joy, Discover, Learn, and Teach." Her goal as a leader is to make a bold and purposeful difference in life.

Sharon has over twenty years of international experience in business and industry spanning eighteen countries. She has held staff and line positions in telecommunications, brewing, health care products, and professional services. This experience is built on an educational foundation of a Bachelor of Science degree in Engineering Management with a Psychology minor, followed by an MBA with an emphasis in Organizational Behavior. Wings of Success has clients that range from Fortune 500 companies including Anheuser-Busch Inc. and The Boeing Companies to small businesses and individuals. In addition, Sharon has been an active volunteer leader in the WLP profession since 1997, currently serving on the 2007–2008 ASTD Board of Directors.

Clients and colleagues have described Sharon as a leader, intuitive, intelligent, aware, personable, creative, warm, fun, high-energy, compassionate, and customer-focused. Her engaging presence and excellent facilitation skills quickly build rapport and enable strategic risk-taking and growth. She provides value to her clients by bringing a fresh perspective, passion for workplace learning and performance, a great sense of humor, and realistic guidance accompanied by practical knowledge and skills. Sharon lives just outside of St. Louis, Missouri, on five and a half acres with her two cats, Oompa Loompa, and Willy Wonka.

Sharon Wingron, CPLP, MBA
Wings of Success LLC
St. Louis, MO
Phone: 888.871.1780
E-mail: info@wingsofsuccess.com
www.developPEOPLE.com
www.DiSCLearningSolutions.com
www.brainmodelearning.com
www.sharonwingron.com

Chapter 7

LES BROWN

THE INTERVIEW

David E. Wright (Wright)

Today we're talking with Les Brown, internationally recognized speaker and CEO of Les Brown Enterprises, Inc. He is also author of the highly acclaimed and successful books, *Live Your Dreams* and *It's Not Over Until You Win*. Les is former host of the *Les Brown Show*, a nationally syndicated daily television talk show that focused on solutions rather than on problems. Les Brown is one of the nation's leading authorities on understanding and stimulating human potential. Utilizing powerful delivery and newly emerging insights, Les's customized presentations will teach, inspire, and channel any audience to new levels of achievement.

Les Brown, welcome to *Rising to the Top: A Guide to Success.*

Les Brown (Brown)

Thank you very much. It's a pleasure to be here.

Wright

Les, you've been a role model for thousands of people down through the years because of your triumph over adversity. Tell our readers a little bit about your early life and who was responsible for your upbringing.

Brown

Well, I was born in a poor section of Miami, Florida, called Liberty City. I was born on the floor of an abandoned building along with a twin brother. When we were six weeks of age, we were adopted. When I was in the fifth grade I was identified as EMR (Educable Mentally Retarded) and put back into the fourth grade. I failed again when I was in the eighth grade.

I attribute everything that I've accomplished to my mother. Whenever I give a presentation I always quote Abraham Lincoln by saying, "All that I am and all that I ever hope to be, I owe to my mother." I saw a sign once that said, "God took me out of my biological mother's womb and placed me in the heart of my adopted mother." I love my adopted mother's faith, her character, her drive, her dedication, and her willingness to do whatever it took to raise seven children by herself. She only had a third grade education but she had a Ph.D. in mothering.

Wright

If I remember correctly, you were diagnosed at the age of thirty-six with dyslexia. How did that happen?

Brown

No, I was never diagnosed with dyslexia; but I was in special education from fourth grade all the way through my senior year in high school. My formal education ended at that time; but I became very much interested in personal development tapes and books because of a high school teacher who challenged me to do something in a class. I told him I couldn't do it and he insisted that I could.

Finally, I said, "I can't because I'm Educable Mentally Retarded."

He said, "Don't ever say that again. Someone's opinion of you does not have to become your reality."

This teacher's name was Mr. Leroy Washington and he's still around today. One of the things he emphasized to all of his students was that you don't get in life what you *want*—you get in life what you *are*. What you achieve—what you produce in life—is a reflection of your growth and development as a person. So you must invest in yourself.

He often quoted scripture by saying, "Be ye not conformed to this world: but be ye transformed by the renewing of your mind . . . " (Romans 12:2). He said most people fail in life because "they don't know that they don't know and they think they know"—they suffer from mental malnutrition. He said take the time each day to develop your mind, read ten to fifteen pages of something positive every day, and find some goals that are beyond your comfort zone that can challenge you to reinvent yourself. He told his students that in order to do something you've never done, you've got to be someone you've never been. He told us the possibilities of what you could achieve by developing your mind and developing your communication skills (because once you open your mouth you tell the world who you are). You can really begin to climb the ladder of success and do things that will literally amaze you.

Wright

So your education is self-education.

Brown

Yes.

Wright

Listening to tapes and reading books and that sort of thing?

Brown

Yes. Going to seminars and then testing and experimenting. I think it's very important that people experiment with their lives and find out what it is that works for them—what gives their lives a sense of joy and meaning. What is it that brings music to your life? That way you're able to discover some talents, abilities, and skills you don't even realize you have.

Wright

I remember reading your first book, *Live Your Dreams*. This bestseller is helping people even today. Can you tell us what you're trying to say in this book and why it is important?

Brown

What I'm doing in *Live Your Dreams* is challenging people to look at their situation and ask themselves some crucial questions. Is life working for me? Is it really giving me what I want?

When most people get out of high school, they end up doing things that other people want them to do. Albert Schweitzer was asked a question, "What's wrong with humankind today?" He replied, "Men simply don't think." He meant that statement in a generic sense. Men *and* women simply don't challenge themselves to think about what it is that really makes them happy and gives their lives a sense of meaning, purpose, power, and value.

I want to challenge people to think about what it is that really gives their lives a sense of meaning and power. Once you determine that, assess yourself. What are your strengths? What are your weaknesses? What is it you bring to the table of life? What help? What assistance? What training? What education? What resources? What do you have to tap into that will help you to become the kind of person that can produce those results?

Then next is to commit yourself. Don't ask yourself, "How am I going to do it?" The "how" is none of your business—what is most important is to get started—the how will come. The way will come. Everything you need to attract—the people, the resources, and the assistance—will come to be available at your disposal.

Wright

What do you think about goal-setting? There has been so much written about it lately.

Brown

I think it's very important that people set goals because what that does is allow you to focus your energy. It helps you to put together a game plan and a strategy and an agenda for your life. If you don't have an agenda for your life, then you're going to be a part of somebody else's agenda; therefore, you want to set some goals. There's a quote I love very much that says, "People who aim at nothing in life usually hit nothing dead on the head."

Wright

Oh, my.

Brown

Yes, so you want to have some goals you are setting in each area of your life. You want to monitor those goals after you put together a plan of action to achieve those goals. Break those goals down into manageable increments: long-range and short-range goals, three-month goals, thirty-day goals, and weekly goals. You should have daily tasks and activities you engage in that will move you in the direction of your goals. Dr. Robert H. Schuller said something that is true, "By the yard it's hard, but inch by inch anything is a cinch."

As you begin to look at the big picture and come back to where you are right now, looking at the completed big picture of where you want to go, then you can begin to put together a strategy of things and activities you need to do each day to move you in the direction of those goals. As you get closer to those goals you have set for yourself in the various areas of your life—your physical life, your emotional life, your spiritual life, your financial life—then you can begin to push the goals back. Continue to stretch—continue to push yourself—and reach farther.

Wright

A few years ago you had a nationally syndicated television talk show. It's next to impossible to get a show of that nature on the air. Tell us the circumstances that helped to get your show on the air.

Brown

I believe I'm coming back, I don't think it's impossible to get back on again. I wanted to go in a different direction. During the time I ventured into it, television was based upon a formula the executives were accustomed to which they'd always implemented—the show must be based upon conflict and controversy. So you had Phil Donahue, Oprah Winfrey, Sally Jesse Raphael, and Geraldo. My show was based upon solutions. I believed you could have a show that was not based upon conflict and controversy—you could have a show where you would look at what challenges people are facing and who has gone through a challenge and come out on the other side? Talk to that person and find out how he or she got there. Interview a guest who is in the middle of a challenge and find one who's just approaching that challenge. Have an expert work the person through that process during the hour of the show, asking what is it that brought you here? There's an old saying that goes, "Wherever you find yourself, at some point and time, you made an appointment to get there."

The other thing is that success leaves clues. What we must do is talk to someone who's had the same problem you've had and find out from his or her experience what is it you can do to implement a game plan. What help and support will you need to work through this problem?

The *Les Brown Show* was very successful. It was the highest rated and fastest cancelled talk show in the history of television. It was cancelled because, even though it had successful ratings, the producers of the show wanted me to do a show based upon conflict and controversy and sensationalism—fathers who sleep with their fourteen-year-old daughter's boyfriends—and subjects like that. I decided to be true to my concept and not venture off into those other areas to do those Jerry Springer type shows, so they cancelled the show and brought someone else in who was willing to cooperate with what they wanted.

Wright

Did you learn any lessons from your highly competitive talk show?

Brown

Yes I did. The lesson I learned was I should have been the executive producer. I was hired talent and "the hand that pays the piper calls the tune." Had I been the executive producer of my show like Oprah Winfrey, then I could have done what Oprah did after she saw the success of my show—she changed direction and used the formula I'd come up with and the rest is history.

If I had it to do over again I would've put my own production company together, continued to do the show I was doing, and would've found someone else to syndicate the show nationally. If I couldn't find someone to syndicate the show nationally I would've set it up to do it locally and then rolled it back out nationally myself.

Wright

I bet you still get stopped on the street by people who saw your commercials on the PBS station for many years. Those were some of the best produced I've ever seen.

Brown

Well, thank you. We've gotten a lot of response from PBS. We just did one show four months ago called, *It's in Your Hands*. In fact, I end the show with my children because five of my seven children are speakers as well; they're also trainers. What we're doing is teaching people how to become responsible for their careers, their health, and for their family life. The response has been very, very successful on PBS.

Wright

So you're growing your own speakers, then.

Brown

Yes, and I'm training speakers—I'm more of a speech coach. I've developed a reputation as a speaker, but I have a gift of helping people tell their story and to position it so it has value for an audience. I have people's stories create special, magical moments within the context of their presentation so that those stories can create a committed listening audience and move them to new heights within themselves.

Wright

Yes, you don't have to tell me you're a sought after speaker. Some time ago we were planning a speaking engagement in Ohio and the two people who were requested more than any others were Stephen Covey and Les Brown. They really came after you, so you do have quite a reputation for helping people.

Brown

Thank you.

Wright

A lot of our readers have read many books that advocate focus in their career. I know you've done several things and you've done them well. Do you advocate going in one direction and not diversifying in your career?

Brown

I think that you have to find one area you want to focus on and as you develop momentum in that area and reach a certain measure of success, then you can branch off into other areas.

Wright

Les, you had a serious bout with cancer several years ago, right?

Brown

Yes.

Wright

How did this catastrophic disease affect your life?

Brown

What cancer did for me was help me live life with a sense of urgency that tomorrow is not guaranteed. It helped me reprioritize my life and find out what's really important. When something major like cancer happens in your life you spend more time focusing on those things. So, even though I always practiced and advocated that people live each day as if it were their last, my cancer battle helped me to focus even more so on priorities. That's what I began to be about the business of doing—thinking about my legacy, spending more time with my children, my grandchildren, friends I cared about, and working on the purpose I've embraced for my life.

Wright

My wife was going through cancer at the same time you were, I remember. I heard her say recently that even though she doesn't want cancer again, she wouldn't give anything for the lessons she learned going through it.

Brown

Yes. It helps; it gives new meaning to life, and you value things you used to take for granted.

Wright

So, you gained a lot of insight into what's important?

Brown

Oh, without any question I did.

Wright

Your book, *It's Not Over Until You Win*, was long awaited, of course. Would you tell our readers what it's about and what you're trying to say?

Brown

I think what people must do is challenge themselves to overcome the inner conversation that has been placed in them through their conditioning, through their environment, and their circumstances. We live in a world where we're told more about our limitations rather than our potential. We need to overcome and defeat that conversation.

If you ask most people if they have ever been told they can't achieve a goal they envision for their life will say, "Yes." My whole goal is to help people learn how to become unstoppable. Yes, it's going to be difficult—it's going to be hard. You're going to have obstacles thrown in your path. You will have setbacks and disappointments. But you must develop the mind-set of a winner. You must come back again and again and again. You must be creative and flexible, versatile and adaptable, and never stop until you reach your goals.

Wright

I read many years ago that 98 percent of all failure comes from quitting. Would you agree with that?

Brown

Yes, I agree with that without any question. Most people become discouraged and they see delay as a denial. I encourage people to go back to the drawing board in their minds, regroup, and get some fresh thinking. Einstein said, "The thinking that has brought me this far has created some problems that this thinking can't solve."

Sometimes we have to allow other people to be a part of the process—to look at the situation we're battling with new eyes that can help us overcome the challenges we're facing.

Wright

As I have said before, you have been a role model for thousands of adults as well as young people. Do you have any advice to give our readers that would help them to grow in body, mind, and spirit and live a better, fuller life?

Brown

Yes. I think it's important for people to raise the bar on themselves every day. Look at your life and understand and know you are greater than you give yourself credit for being; you have talents and abilities you haven't even begun to reach for yet.

Jim Rohn has a quote I love, "When the end comes for you, let it find you conquering a new mountain, not sliding down an old one." So, therefore, we have to raise the bar on ourselves constantly and assess ourselves.

The other thing is I believe it's important we ask for help, not because we're weak but because we want to remain strong. Many people don't ask for help because of pride. "Pride cometh before a fall" because of ego. E-G-O means edging God out.

I think that you also have to ask yourself, what is your plan for being here? Most people take their health for granted; but living a long, healthy life is not a given—pain is a given—you have to fight to stay here. You have to have a plan of action to stay here. So what is your plan for being here? Put yourself on your to-do list. Develop a plan of action on how you're going to take better care of yourself and spend more time with people you care about. Focus on living the goals and dreams you've envisioned for yourself that are the calling on your life.

Wright

Down through the years, as you've made your decisions, has faith played an important role in your life?

Brown

Yes, faith is very important. I think you have to believe in yourself, believe in your abilities, believe in your dreams, and believe in a power greater than yourself. There's a quote I love which says, "Faith is the oil that takes the friction out of living." Do the best you can and leave the rest to a power greater than yourself.

Wright

Les, you don't know how much I appreciate you being with us today on *The Power of Motivation*.

Brown

Oh, thank you so much.

Wright

Today we've been talking with Les Brown, an internationally recognized speaker and CEO of Les Brown Enterprises. He's the author of *Live Your Dreams* and *It's Not Over Until You Win*. I suggest you run down to the bookstore and look for both of them. Les has been a successful talk show host and as we have heard today, he is now coaching speakers.

Thank you so much for being with us, Les.

Brown

Thank you, I appreciate you very much.

About The Author

Les Brown is an internationally recognized speaker and CEO of Les Brown Enterprises, Inc. He is also author of the highly acclaimed and successful books, *Live Your Dreams* and *It's Not Over Until You Win*. Les Brown is one of the nation's leading authorities in understanding and stimulating human potential.

Les Brown Enterprises
PO Box 27380
Detroit, Michigan 48227
Phone: 800.733.4226
E-mail: speak@lesbrown.com
www.lesbrown.com

Chapter 8

VIDUSHI BABBER, MD

David Wright (Wright)

Today we're talking with Vidushi Babber, MD, a medical director, speaker, educator, author, physician, beauty queen, and talk show host.

You certainly have risen to the top of your profession. Would you tell our readers a little about your background and why you chose the medical profession?

Vidushi Babber, MD (Babber)

Entering the medical profession was my parents' dream—more my mother's as she had wanted to become a physician herself, which happened to be her father's dream. It was a family desire that never had been fulfilled until I was born, and then the journey to have a doctor in the family began.

When I entered college I began studying toward a degree in biology; but found I also enjoyed psychology quite a bit, so I majored in both.

By the time I began medical school, I knew I would specialize in psychiatry as my choice for residency training. After all, the equation was simple: Psychology + Medicine = Psychiatry. The decision was solidified when, at the end of my last psychiatric rotation in medical school, I encountered a patient who had never smiled in the last twenty years he had been institutionalized.

I worked with him daily—therapy sessions, medication adjustments, etc.—for one month. I kept smiling at him the entire time, but he never smiled back.

Three days before the end of my rotation he asked to speak with me. He sat in a chair across from me in the evaluation room and began to sing. The part that was so memorable about that was some of the lyrics of the song he sang: "... how smiling makes your sorrows go away ... " And at the end of the song, he smiled. I smiled back, knowing I was on the right track with him and in my own life.

Wright

While researching your practice and specialties, I read that depression is the leading cause of disability worldwide. Is that true?

Babber

It is unfortunately true. I had never realized the severity of depression as a disability until I began practicing two years ago. In school and training quite often we are wrapped up in learning how to take care of patients and we are not that exposed to the paperwork and documentation needed for disability and medical leave. Our attending physicians or mentors would be responsible for those things. When it came time to complete these forms myself, I began to notice the increase of paperwork I had to do each week. It came to the point where nearly every other day I was working on disability and medical leave paperwork. That was when I heard the alarm go off in my head. For the past year I have been researching the effect of depression, not only across the nation, but worldwide—it was shocking.

I then began to create seminars and talks addressing this global issue and I am currently working on a book titled, *Depression is My Business.*

Wright

I also read that decreased productivity and absenteeism because of depression costs employers $50 billion annually and the treatment costs are greater than $10 billion each year. Are corporations aware of that fact?

Babber

I wish more of them were—if they were, I do not believe these numbers would be so high. It was not until I began my own clinical practice that my patients began sharing the effect their depression was having in their workplaces.

In order to help them, I began to find resources about dealing with depression while working. I only came across one book and that was written years ago. It was disheartening to learn that an illness causing so much personal grief was also affecting our economy. I wondered what as a society are we doing about it?

I could not locate many resources or explanations other than statistics about depression affecting the workplace so I began to try to understand the cycle myself in order to educate others about it. I began defining workplace depression with my "depressee versus depressor" theory and how it related to the employee and employer relationship.

Wright

In *A Healthier You!*, a book you co-authored with some of America's leading health and fitness experts, you wrote, "Pregnancy marks the stage of many emotions in a women's life. Happiness and excitement are responses a mother is expected to experience. Unfortunately, this may not always be the case. Pregnancy also may be perceived as a stressful life event leading to psychiatric disorders, which unfortunately are overlooked and often dismissed."

How does this effect a women's ability to "get back in the race" toward success and her pursuit of rising to the top of her profession?

Babber

For some reason, women are expected to always be the perfect wife, the perfect mother, and in this day and age, the perfect career woman. Often it is this expectation that prevents these women from accepting themselves, no matter how "imperfect" they feel they are. And they need to realize that just as life is imperfect, so are they. When the pressure to be perfect is removed, they will start living life and finding success. Until then they're only racing against their own creation of their "perfect" self, which will lead to personal and professional difficulties.

The same principle applies to the expectations of feeling happy and excited during pregnancy. Women need to express themselves regardless of their perception of themselves or others. What's the point of creating the happiness bubble if sooner or later it will pop? When it does they're left in an unfortunate situation that may endanger themselves or their baby.

When people live freely, work freely, and express freely, they don't need to make such an effort to rise, they will easily float to the top.

Wright

You are also involved in PageantDoc. Will you tell our readers how you got involved in pageants and why you do it?

Babber

I'm glad you asked this question because it's one many people quite often wonder about. I believe it's because they don't really imagine a physician competing in pageants, especially a physician who is running a successful practice and who is a medical director, as I am.

Although I do not fit the mold of the typical physician, I connect better with my patients. I'm a "real" person with real hobbies and real desires. My life does not revolve around my career, which is only one aspect of my life. Everyone is blessed with many talents and passions and there is no reason why one cannot pursue different interests.

I participate in pageants as others would play sports—a pageant is an event you train for and compete in. What better way to practice poise, articulation, and self-presentation? The best feeling for me is being able to display the true essence of a woman's beauty—knowledge—when I am given the opportunity to speak my mind answering the on-stage question.

It was this experience, along with my profession, that at the end of fifteen years led me to PageantDoc. I imagined that if I placed all my qualities, interests, education, and dreams in a blender and had to create my own "smoothie," what would I call it? The first thing that popped in my head was PageantDoc. I quickly learned that I was beginning to blend out instead of blending in. I enjoyed it because I was comfortable and happy—it was okay to do it my way.

Wright

Let's talk about some of your interests in women's health. Your seminar topics include eating disorders, abuse, domestic violence, and rape trauma. These problems are reported in the news media every day. What are you doing to help alleviate these atrocities?

Babber

The answer to this is The Winning Doc Enterprise, which includes PageantDoc and my show, *Winning with Wellness: Where Beauty Meets Health.* The programs were created to enhance the education of wellness and address these and other societal concerns and issues. We need to be aware of problems and be educated properly before we can solve them. This is why we go to school.

I have been fortunate to have patients who open up and tell me that they wish they had known about the life situations that were negatively affecting their emotional and mental health. They felt that their families, communities, and schools had never taught them how to take care of themselves.

As a society we become side-tracked in raising children to be successful in academics, sports, and their careers. We forget that true success includes a healthy state of mind. When we feel emotionally and mentally balanced, we've then set the foundation for life-long success. In order for this to be attained, we need to educate people about mental health, which will bring awareness into their lives. They will then be able to help themselves and others. Until society as a whole does not grasp this concept, mental health issues will continue to be major a topic in the news media.

Wright

Why the name, The Winning Doc?

Babber

The name defines and represents myself and what I would like to educate people about achieving within themselves—to bring out their winning abilities—to *"Win from WithIN"!* Plus it represents a role model both adults and children can relate to—a positive influence where the message is "Smart is Beautiful."

Wright

What is the format of your *Winning with Wellness* show and how do you help women feel good and look good?

Babber

Winning with Wellness brings to listeners a regular educational program on women's issues. We often hear of some particular topic on the news or a subject that a talk show has covered, but there has never been a program that addresses these concerns on a regular basis. This show is the answer to that educational need.

I have carefully formatted it to cover several aspects. The most important aspect is "wellness." I define "wellness" as looking and feeling good—a perfect win-win situation! This will eventually lead to "doing good." There are several guests and several segments. We always include a "wellness" guest who is a national leader, physician, author, or speaker who champions women's health and beauty.

Our "Super Role Model" segment highlights the accomplishment of a woman in the community who is promoting wellness in our society.

Our "Winner's Edge" segment is to encourage the entrepreneurial spirit. Women have always taken care of business inside the home and have been trained to be the CEOs of their households. This segment showcases those women who have stepped outside of their home to create their own businesses and their own financial freedom. It serves as a launch pad for these women who are creating and offering various wellness and beauty products and services, from the latest to the greatest.

So before these women appear on Jay, David, Larry, or the famous "O" show, my show will feature them first. If you've noticed, we've wrapped the show very nicely into a total package of winning with wellness.

Wright

You've certainly achieved quite a bit so early in life. Will you share with our readers more about the success you've experienced in helping to guide others?

Babber

When I entered college at sixteen I really didn't expect that I would become a medical director fifteen years later. I realize that I may have had somewhat of a head start compared to my peers but that didn't mean things came easily. I too had my share of personal struggles.

One's dreams and accomplishments should not be measured by a yardstick others use—create your own.

This reminds me of times when I would tell my father my expectations about how old I would be and when I would achieve certain goals. It may sound surprising but I'm on track—according to my own yardstick.

For others, this may be too fast or too slow. There will always be people who have achieved more or less than I have achieved. Does it really matter? As long as I am going at my own comfortable pace and learning from my experiences, I will reach success.

You almost have to become an expert in small failures before you earn your right to big success. Achieving success is like a trampoline—until you come down, how will you know how far and how much higher you can really go up the next time? And by the way, the limit is higher than just the sky.

Wright

Finally Dr. Babber, what can the ordinary person—one who doesn't have your medical training—do to help this nation be more aware of problems that diminish our ability to be successful and rise to the top?

Babber

We need to first educate the people of this nation on the five principles of being HAPPY so they can be successful and rise to the top:

Hold on to your dreams—If you let go, they won't come true.
Always love yourself—More and more each day.
Passion and Persistence—These are no longer "secret" ingredients; use them.
Please lift, not drift—Join forces and go higher; forget the competition; coincide, not divide.
You can do it!—Believe, conceive, and achieve and you will.

And always remember what your Winning Doc says: *"Where there's wellness there's a win!"*

About the Author

VIDUSHI BABBER, MD currently serves as Medical Director and has a private practice at The Institute for Neuropsychiatry in Louisiana. Her expertise is in women's mental health issues including pregnancy and post-partum mood disorders, domestic violence, eating disorders, and trauma. Dr. Babber is a graduate of St. George's University School of Medicine. She began her psychiatry residency at Loyola University, Illinois, and continued her training at the University of Texas Medical Branch in Galveston. She graduated with a fellowship in Women's Mental Health from the University of Illinois in Chicago.

Dr. Babber is well-known for her advocacy in prevention and education of psychiatric disorders. She has been a recognized faculty member and a favorite among medical students and residents leading to several teaching awards. She is highly requested for conferences, quoted in newspapers, frequently interviewed on radio and television including *Ask the Expert* on KPLC-TV, and also hosts her own talk show, *Winning With Wellness: Where Beauty Meets Health*. Dr. Babber has co-authored *A Healthier You* (available at www.drbabber.com) featuring Deepak Chopra and Billy Blanks. Her latest pursuit is authoring two upcoming books, *Winning with Wellness* and *Depression is My Business.*

Dr. Babber knows the power of a woman! With nearly fifteen years of pageant experience, she has been both a competitor and titleholder in ten pageants. As medical director and a psychiatrist with expertise in women's mental health, Dr. Babber has made her mark, becoming one of the first mental health experts in the nation to combine a platform of beauty along with mind and body wellness. She has been instrumental in the creation of The Winning Doc Enterprise designed to educate on mental, physical, emotional, and spiritual health and has founded PageantDoc, a venue for providing pageant contestants with mental health education. Dr. Babber, aka, "The Winning Doc," has certainly become quite a global phenomenon as an international mind, body, and beauty expert.

Vidushi Babber, MD
The Winning Doc Enterprise
Phone: 800.573.7351
Fax: 866.538.6982
www.drbabber.com
www.winningdoc.com
www.pageantdoc.com

Chapter 9

KENNETH N. IVORY, MBA, FMP, CFBE

THE INTERVIEW

David Wright (Wright)

Kenneth N. Ivory, MBA, FMP, CFBE, is a dynamic international motivational speaker, enthusiastic trainer, high impact facilitator, and visionary leader. His illustrious professional career spans over twenty years in the hospitality, academic, and non-profit industries. His professional credentials include Certified Food and Beverage Executive by the American Hotel and Lodging Association, Food Management Professional by the National Restaurant Association, member of the Institute of Hospitality of the United Kingdom, certified personality temperament facilitator, certified learning facilitator for Carlton Advanced Management Institute, certified facilitator for Achieve Global, a visiting faculty member in the Department of Hospitality and Tourism Administration in the School of Business at North Carolina Central University, and a Professional Member of the National Speakers Association.

Ken, welcome to *Rising to the Top: A Guide to Success.*

Kenneth Ivory (Ivory)
Thank you.

Wright
Kenneth, I know you've heard many, many definitions of success, but how do *you* define success?

Ivory
Well David, I define success as a very unique formula. I believe that $D + D + P^2$ = Success. Determination + Discipline + Passion^2 = Success. It takes "Determination" to be successful. You cannot allow your past to dictate your present. You cannot allow past circumstances to determine your future outcome.

Growing up in a "single parent" home, in a small rural town in Georgia, I was "determined" to not become a "product" of my circumstances—growing up without a father. I was determined to get an education and with the unwavering support of my mother, my church, community leaders, and great teachers throughout my elementary and high school years, I was fortunate to achieve my academic ambitions.

The second part of the equation is "Discipline." Great athletes, great performers, and great leaders are successful because they are disciplined. When I refer to discipline I am referring to a "holistic" approach to discipline. You must be disciplined in your mind, body, and spirit and have a "focus-driven lifestyle." Your attitude must be disciplined, your character and integrity must be disciplined, and your life balance must be disciplined.

It has taken discipline for me to achieve my lifelong dreams and aspirations. Growing up in a small town I always dreamed of being on stage. I enjoyed presenting at churches and schools so I knew I had a gift, but it had to be developed. Jim Collins highlights this concept in his book, *Good to Great.* In the book he wrote about a marathon athlete who "rinses his cottage cheese" to remove the fat that is left. We need to have the same tenacity and perseverance about our life goals and aspirations.

The next component of this key to success is "Passion." I believe that without the "fire of passion" burning inside it is challenging to achieve success. That is the reason why passion is "squared" in the formula I gave, not just doubled. It takes more than just twice as much passion to be successful—it takes an exponential commitment to achieve your life's dreams and aspirations. Passion drives you to go beyond your limits, excel, and achieve the impossible.

I started my leadership and consulting firm in 1998 with no money or any other resources, just a dream of having my name on business cards. I can recall my wife and I doing the Internet research necessary to understand how to incorporate a business in the State of North Carolina, how to start a home-based business, and even how to create a Web site. We were determined to start a company. We looked back at our formula $D + D + P^2 =$ Success and made it happen.

My success is not based on the accolades and personal possessions I have accumulated throughout my career—it is based on the many people whose lives I have enriched and empowered and my having been able to give people hope and plant a seed for them to be successful using such a simple, yet powerful formula.

Wright

What would you say has been the biggest contribution to your professional success?

Ivory

The biggest contribution to my professional success, besides the many mentors and coaches I have encountered in my professional career, are my family and my strong spiritual foundation. My success would not have even been possible without the steadfast support of my family and without a strong spiritual foundation.

My mother has always been the driving force in pushing me to excel beyond my expectations. My wife has continued that unwavering support. She has spent countless days reviewing my research papers and case studies while working toward my MBA degree and now as I pursue my PhD in Human Environmental Sciences with a concentration in Hospitality and Tourism Administration. We stayed up all night on Mother's Day in 1999 to launch my Web site.

In my opinion, I believe that every successful person needs a support mechanism to achieve greatness—someone to encourage you, keep you focused, someone to be "brutally" honest with you, someone to collaborate thoughts and ideas, and keep the momentum of your spirit moving forward.

My spiritual foundation keeps me humble and grounded to always give thanks to God for all things and be a blessing to others.

Wright

Aside from personal role models, who are the people who have served as your role models for success?

Ivory

Other role models include former President Jimmy Carter. I was fortunate to have grown up only twenty-eight miles northwest of Plains, Georgia, and privileged to be acquainted with his extended family through 4-H activities and Mr. Murray Smith, President Carter's brother-in-law, who was my high school algebra teacher. Even through his trials and tribulations during his presidency, he maintained steadfast in his faith in God, his character, and his integrity.

Other powerful role models include: Dr. Maya Angelou, Les Brown, Bill Cosby, Dave Ramsey, Dr. Johnnetta B. Cole, and Dr. John C. Maxwell.

Wright

What do you think are the biggest obstacles people face in trying to become successful?

Ivory

The biggest obstacle people face in trying to become successful is that they do not have a vision. There is a significant difference between having an idea and a vision. Helen Keller once said, "The only thing worse than being blind is having sight but no vision." Ideas are a variety of thoughts and concepts, and they may not come to fruition. People come up with great ideas, but some are never executed. However, with a vision you are focused, and every executable concept that you make can come alive. Having a "vision" is the cornerstone for success. You must have "laser-beam" focus to bring your vision to reality.

In addition, most people must have passion to drive them to success. Ken Hemphill once said, ". . . vision does not ignite growth, passion does. Passion fuels vision and vision is the focus of the power of passion. Leaders who are passionate about their call create vision." Most people are not as self-disciplined as that and therefore cannot fulfill their vision.

Wright

Would you tell our readers a little bit about what drives you to be successful?

Ivory

What drives me to be successful is an insatiable desire to be a servant-leader. I believe that my purpose in life is to empower and enlighten the best in people. Because of the many great people who shaped and molded me for greatness, I must give back to others and help them reach their unlimited potential. I must inspire others so they too can reach their dreams.

I can look back at my childhood and visualize all those who coached and mentored me. I have a desire to share with others. I'm driven by the lack of role models for our young people today. I'm driven by the fact that one must be a "trailblazer" for others to follow.

I have been fortunate in being able to share with young people in detention centers, to energetic and impressionable students on Native American reservations in Wyoming. I've listened to them talk about what they want to be when they grow up and things they want to do in life. What drives me to be successful is being able to help them reach their goals.

I spoke at Wind River High School in Pavilion, Wyoming, and the students were outstanding. I talked about changing their behavior to be successful. I received very touching handwritten notes from many, many students who shared with me how they changed their behavior. Some changes included their behavior toward their parents, some were going to clean up their rooms more often, and some were going to focus and study harder in school and change their "attitude" about school. This drives me to continue my quest to be successful.

One of my college students at North Carolina Central University was having some personal problems with an organization that he was having difficulty resolving. This tall, tough guy was a bit "shy" so he slipped me a personal note by placing it on my desk. He wrote, "This is my first experience with a faculty member that cares so much for the students. It makes me proud to be associated with a department that puts students' priorities first."

Wright

Is it important to balance your success in your life? If so, how do you balance your success with your life?

Ivory

Without life balance you cannot be successful. I learned this lesson the hard way. As a young professional in the hospitality industry, I was driven to succeed. My aspirations were not limited to being a

Food Service Manager—I wanted to be the Director of Food Services, then District Manager, and then a Vice President. Climbing the corporate ladder was earned at a high cost. I accepted a dynamic opportunity to serve as Vice President of Operations for a progressive food service management firm in New Jersey. I was excited about this executive-level opportunity. This transition happened during school time, therefore my family remained in Durham, North Carolina, and I headed to Florham Park, New Jersey. My son was two years old and my daughter was eight years old at the time.

I enjoyed the fast-paced challenges as a Vice President, however my family was suffering. My son became seriously ill; my focus made a drastic change and I had to make a decision. As a result, I returned to Durham because my family's needs became my priority. This also opened the doors for me to start my consulting firm as well as assist my senior pastor, Luther K. Brooks, in executing his vision to revitalize the Walltown Community.

To have balance with work and life, I must set priorities with my family as well as my travel and consulting schedule. My bishop's wife looked me square in the eyes at an extravagant catering showcase and said, "When are you going to take a vacation?" She didn't mean just a "family vacation" to have fun and relax, but to re-energize, refocus, and look at my life's priorities and commit to developing my family with the same passion as I have done in developing others.

Wright

What is the message that you want people to hear so that they can learn from your success?

Ivory

The message I want others to hear is that first of all, success is achievable by your own definition of success, whether its fame or fortune or healthy living. Secondly, to be successful you should follow my formula: Determination + Discipline + Passion^2 = Success. Third, you cannot allow your circumstances or shortcomings to hinder you from achieving success. Where you start in life from birth does not determine where you will end. Success has a "price tag," what are you willing to pay? What are you willing to sacrifice to achieve it?

Wright

You speak about passion being our "guiding principle" for life and that it is the main factor in attaining success. Is passion alone truly enough?

Ivory

No, I wouldn't say that "passion" alone is the answer or total key for attaining success. You must be determined and disciplined to attain that success. Many people sit around their homes and offices and are "passionate" about being successful or they see very successful people executing their vision and they become passionate about it. You can have an untiring, insatiable desire or "passion" to be a prolific orator, but until you discipline yourself and develop your speaking or leadership skills, it's just a "dream deferred."

Wright

We all know what the dictionary definition of passion is, but how do you define it?

Ivory

Passion is an intense, overpowering, relentless drive and/or desire to achieve one's maximum potential or success. It's an unquenchable thirst for excellence.

Wright

How did you begin speaking and why did you choose passion as one of your main topics or area of focus?

Ivory

Actually, my speaking career began in high school when I became the first male State Officer in Georgia of the Future Homemakers of America organization. The notoriety of being the first male state officer in a predominately female organization provided me a platform to share my passion with others from a non-traditional viewpoint.

What catapulted my passion as a speaker was a seminar I attended in the early nineties. I participated in a management training seminar at Walt Disney World Resorts called "Leadership for a Changing World." I became inspired with a concept that dealt with "colors" to describe personality temperament. Because of the "edutainment" component, I enjoyed being entertaining and yet providing a valuable lesson to others. I therefore became a national certification trainer. I started a hospitality leadership training and development firm in the late nineties and the rest is history! Passion is one of my main topics and focus because it is truly a key element in "rising to the top." Passion is a driving force that keeps you up all night dreaming about reaching your maximum potential.

Wright

How did you conclude that speaking was your passion?

Ivory

That happened when I conducted my very first personality temperament training in early 1995 in Atlanta, Georgia. I was excited, yet nervous of my very first "edutainment" experience. The participants were all seated, anticipating the start of another "traditional" facilitating model where they expected the facilitator to "lecture" to them instead of engaging them. I jumped out of the side door adorned in my bright orange bathrobe, wearing "larger than life" orange clown glasses, and a wig—an unforgettable entrance! As I continued my "bathroom robe" monologue, changing from a blue robe to a gold robe, and then to a green robe, the audience was in awe, shocked, surprised, and astonished! At the close of the two-and-one-half-day training, the evaluations from the participants were rave reviews. It gave me such a euphoric feeling to hear people talk about how much I truly changed their lives by allowing them to understand themselves and others through a thorough understanding of the power of personality and temperament.

I have traveled throughout the country and abroad donning my colorful robes and sharing a message about leadership, teambuilding, diversity, customer service, organizational change, and success. From that point forward, I knew unequivocally that I had a powerful message to deliver that absolutely would change the lives of others. Over the years, I have been fortunate to deliver my message to many audiences in which I have changed behaviors, changed attitudes, and motivated and empowered people to reach their maximum potential.

Wright

How would you define leadership?

Ivory

Leadership is the ability to influence without a doubt. Throughout history great leaders, whether their decisions were positive or negative, were extremely influential. They had an ability to "influence" their followers. Leadership is a trait that can be learned or acquired through life's experiences. Leadership is not doing things right, but doing the right things that make an impact. Whether you are trying to build a productive sales team or motivating a team that has lost focus, in the words of Dr. John C. Maxwell, leadership is standing firm during those crucible moments. Leadership is a process that is ultimately concerned with fostering change for the greater good. Leadership represents a "synergistic" relationship among leaders, followers, and measurable outcomes. Leadership connects people to processes, provides strategic direction, builds teams and lasting relationships, and makes effective decisions to accomplish astonishing goals and objectives of any organization.

Wright

Who are your role models and mentors in the speaking industry?

Ivory

Zig Ziglar, Les Brown, Dr. John C. Maxwell, Dr. Ken Blanchard, Bishop T.D. Jakes, and Joel S. Osteen.

Wright

How do you know what you need to be successful?

Ivory

This answer lies in whatever you believe it takes for you to be successful. If your goal is to be a successful lawyer, you must successfully graduate from law school, successfully complete the bar exam, and build a clientele. If success for you is measured in wealth-building, you need the support and guidance of successful financial advisors or investment specialists. If you have a passion to start your own business, you must have an entrepreneurial spirit. If you have a desire to be successful in the speaking, training, facilitating, or consulting business, you must be articulate, have a compelling message to share, be able to invoke change in people's lives, find your niche market, and learn from the best in our field.

Wright

How did you get interested in the hospitality industry?

Ivory

Well, actually it was a choice of an elective in my first year of high school in the eighth grade. I had a chance to sign up for shop or home economics. I didn't want to carve my name in wood, so I decided to learn how to make "biscuits" with the girls. I had a great teacher, Mrs. Deborah Ford, who coached and mentored me in home economics and I got very involved in the Future Homemakers of America organization. I became interested in the food service industry and received scholarships to attend Abraham Baldwin Agricultural College, the University of Georgia, and the rest is history!

I graduated from the University of Georgia and accepted my first hospitality management position in Durham, North Carolina. My career spans more than twenty years of serving in the roles of Food Service Manager, Human Resources Manager, Retail Operations Manager, Area Manager, Regional Operations Specialists, Executive Director, District Manager, Vice President of Business Operations, Vice President of Operations, and now President/CEO of Ivory Management Group, Inc.

Wright

Who are some of great leaders and mentors you have encountered in your chosen industry?

Ivory

I have been fortunate to be coached and mentored by some of the greatest leaders the hospitality industry has to offer. A few who impacted my success in the industry include: Senator Larry Shaw and Evelyn Shaw of Shaw Food Services, Johnny Rivers of Walt Disney World Resorts, Bill Hall of Marriott Educational Services, Dean Savas of Motel 6, and James Taylor of Sodexho USA.

Wright

What made them great leaders and mentors?

Ivory

They were human, personable, great coaches and mentors who provided honest and candid feedback. They provided me with opportunities for personal growth and development, and allowed me to reach my potential. They were leaders of high character, integrity, unquestionable ethics, and an insatiable belief in their people. They were visionary and transformational leaders. They had a clear view of the vision, personal commitment to the vision, brought others to the vision, and inspired others to grasp the vision. They accepted responsibility, were accountable for their actions, took action, lead by example, and served as a sounding board. They were great communicators and earned the respect of their followers and peers. They were the epitome of true leadership during prosperous times and they had a resolute character during turbulent times within the organization.

About the Author

KENNETH N. IVORY, MBA, FMP, CFBE, is a dynamic international motivational speaker, enthusiastic trainer, high impact facilitator, and visionary leader. His illustrious professional career spans over twenty years in the hospitality, academic, and non-profit industries. His professional credentials include Certified Food and Beverage Executive by the American Hotel and Lodging Association, Food Management Professional by the National Restaurant Association, member of the Institute of Hospitality of the United Kingdom, certified personality temperament facilitator, certified learning facilitator for Carlton Advanced Management Institute, a certified facilitator for Achieve Global, a visiting faculty member in the Department of Hospitality and Tourism Administration in the School of Business at North Carolina Central University, and a Professional Member of the National Speakers Association.

Kenneth N. Ivory, MBA, FMP, CFBE
Kenneth Ivory, LLC
604 Southshore Parkway, Suite J
Durham, NC 27703
Phone: 919.596.1325
www.kennethivory.com

Chapter 10

BERT FIFE

David Wright (Wright)

Today we are speaking with Bert Fife. Speaking and writing from her own experience, Bert McCoy Fife made an unexpected 360-degree turn from dental hygienist to in-store marketing entrepreneur. As you discover how her rise to the top has a much deeper personal meaning, you may be inspired to pay attention to the signals that it's time for a change for you and to summon the courage and resources to do it. You may reach Bert by e-mail at Bert@bertfife.com to make arrangements for her to speak to your business or organization about topics that will help you and your employees to grow individually and as a team.

Bert, welcome to *Rising to the Top: A Guide to Success.*

Bert Fife (Fife)

Thank you.

Wright

What does "rising to the top" mean to you?

Fife

Sometimes I think "the top" is just a mirage because every time we think we have arrived, it seems to disappear and we turn to look in another direction.

I would like to talk about my journey of starting my own business, building it, and selling it. That is where I have experience.

Wright

How did your journey begin?

Fife

As a dental hygienist, I thought I was pretty good at it. I had a good, growing practice in a group with more than one dentist. Unfortunately there seemed to be a disturbance between two of the dentists. One of them came in and shot the other one! I happened to be there at the time and you can imagine how traumatic that was.

In the state of Louisiana a hygienist cannot work without a dentist. I went into a solo practice with another dentist. About a year later he decided that he didn't want to practice dentistry anymore. Suddenly I found myself without a job—again. I had to suddenly stop and consider, "What is the message here for me?"

I love the game of basketball. If you keep your eye on the ball you can usually see where things are going and occasionally you can score. I felt like a basketball bouncing around at that time and I was taking a good look at the bounces.

Wright

You had no training for starting a business and yet you thought you could succeed. How did you get your start?

Fife

I had no training in how to start a business, so I took some time off and reflected on what I needed to do. I went on a cruise—an inexpensive cruise from New Orleans. I met a woman who did what is called "fragrance sampling" and I thought that this is something no one was doing where I lived in Baton Rouge, Louisiana. I decided to come back and see about working in retail department stores, and that is what I did by providing fragrance samplers.

I had been doing this for about four months and one day I was at the office of the secretarial service that I was using in my business. The manager of the service shared an office with a Pillsbury associate and when he walked in I said, "Don't you need someone in the super-market introducing all those new products your company comes out with?"

"Yes we do," he replied.

"Then people can try it before they buy it instead of just buying it because you say it's good."

"Boy, do we ever need that," he said.

Before you know it I was putting together an in-store marketing company.

Wright

What solidified your vision?

Fife

Well, I think that visions can come from observing the market-place and seeing where there is a need and where you can fit into that need.

The talent I have is working with people. I enjoy people and con-necting with them; in-store marketing is a people-to-people industry. Other industries in New Orleans had taken a nosedive and there were a lot of people out of work. I was ready to see how consumers could get more value for their money and only buy the things they had sampled. I knew I could find people to help me who had been dis-placed from their jobs.

In-store marketing seemed like a great match for me; it seemed like something I could do and succeed in.

Wright

What was the purpose of your business?

Fife

The purpose was to allow people to try before they buy. More im-portantly, I think it was just as important to create jobs for people who had a marketable skill. One of the things I had always said was that most people at the time had the experience. If they had tried something they liked in a store and then told their family members and friends about it, they had basically done the equivalent of sam-pling—in-store marketing. People had to do their own sampling every night at the dinner table or at lunch etc. We had to create a great ex-perience in getting people to try a product and convincing them to like it. It was a great opportunity to get local samplers who worked in the stores they shopped in, then the money goes full circle.

Wright

Once your vision was clear, how did you establish a growth plan?

Fife

I soon figured out that in order to promote the business I had to get the message out that what I was offering was a marketing tool for manufacturers. I started meeting with retailers and had to learn the industry. Most people go into stores and they think that the product just jumped onto the shelves. Very few people think about the process of ordering and the supply chain involved in getting products into the stores, how they determine what products make it onto the shelves and remain.

I found out that every month there are a thousand new products introduced into the marketplace—we have a lot to choose from. There is a lot of sampling that can be done to give these products a chance to survive. It was easy, therefore, to get a growth plan.

I determined that I wanted to cover retail outlets in Louisiana and Mississippi. So I wanted to be a small southeast regional agent who presented in-store events. In order to establish a growth plan I had to contact product manufacturers and suppliers to national and local retail chains. My concept was to supply people who lived in the southeast region who knew those who were shopping with them and then create a relationship with them. They knew that they were people of integrity and everyone would get along better if they were with people they knew rather than transferring people within the two-state area and paying for their transportation. We could get people in their own neighborhoods who would be familiar with shoppers, thereby building trust.

Wright

How did your business compare with the current business model in 1986?

Fife

Basically, I was flying by the seat of my pants; but it seemed that I knew what to do. It just made sense to me that this was a viable marketing plan. At the time, businesses didn't really communicate a lot with their people. In 1986 it was a much more exclusive club regarding who ran the business and how the business was run. What I did was open it up and create an organization that communicated freely with its people regarding where the business was going and what our goals were.

Wright

What was your mission for your employees?

Fife

I wanted to share the vision of being the best and to create a business environment that would maximize their visions and talents. Our employees could then work in a company they would really feel good about working for and let it create income. The better we became, the more products we sold and the better relationships we built. We would sometimes do fifteen hundred promotions in a weekend. You need to be in the stores when shoppers are in the stores and that was Friday, Saturday, and Sunday.

In-store marketing is a self-propelling business because once we established a relationship with the manufacturers we would have on-going products we would represent. What we wanted to do was create an environment where people could work freely and where the information flew through the company in a rapid sequence so that we could develop programs. As we went through the process of the business, communication was timely and the sales figures were tallied very quickly so that we could get back to the clients very quickly with data to help determine market challenges and opportunities. It's not only about the customer interface, it's more importantly about the data.

Wright

What was your mission for your clients?

Fife

Our mission was to provide people who would offer samples of the product at the point of purchase. These people were professionals— people who could maximize public acceptance of our clients' products by encouraging consumers to buy the product and then to provide our clients with timely sales information so that they could act upon it quickly and provide better service.

Wright

What were the shared values in your business?

Fife

You know, I think that shared values are critical to a successful business. When you have people in your organization who don't share your values it will be a clog in the wheel on your road to success. We shared the values of honesty and integrity and personal responsibility. When people agreed to be in a store at the exact time they were assigned to be there, their yes had to mean yes and their no had to mean no.

The reason this was so important was because ads had been run and products had been delivered. It was just one more step in the media mix that had taken place in order to make the promotional event successful. Honesty and integrity are integral parts of this. If one of our employees could not be at an in-store promotional event, then there were major steps that had to take place including finding someone else to be there. The trust factor from store managers was critical. Each person entering the store delivered a feedback form with an 800 number to report concerns.

Wright

How did you align people to those values?

Fife

We made mistakes and the fact that we were willing to make them right built trust. We set a zero tolerance for dishonesty—*zero* tolerance. I always believe that like attracts like so everyone from the president to the janitor must model honesty. When honesty is the norm—if someone is not aligned—it becomes very obvious.

Wright

What were the most effective tools you offered in your business?

Fife

I think probably the most effective tools included providing personal and professional growth opportunities for the people who worked within my organization. I also provided them with the opportunity to meet with our clients so that there could be a comfort level with all of them.

We had regular quarterly meetings and workshops. I also published a bi-monthly newsletter. Again, it is that communication from the top so that everyone could be on the same page. It communicated what our challenges were, what our opportunities were, and what our rewards were.

Everyone in the organization took part in the program. We received many national awards from manufacturers for sales excellence and for public relations excellence. Though my name was on the building—Bert Fife and Associates—I did not receive those awards personally. I let the account executive in charge of that project accept the award. Then there was an award program for people out in the field who had done an excellent job. My focus was more on "the Associates" part of our company name. They were continually being recognized for doing a good job.

Once when there was hurricane damage in South Louisiana, the team in Jackson, Mississippi, collected money to send to the associates who suffered losses. That's effective team-building within an organization.

We conducted many sales contests to reward high achievers. In our "Time to Sell" program, samplers could win a company watch. It was fun and exciting for those in-store.

Wright

How has your business impacted the business model today?

Fife

There seems to be more family consideration in the business today. There seems to be more open communication on financial reports, even in private businesses. There seems to be more open communication from people in leadership to those out in the field. That was something else we did that seems to be becoming more popular today.

We had a lot of young mothers working in our office and over the eighteen years I was in business, we had six newborn infants that came to work with either their mother or father. They could come to the office for the first three months, then after three months they went into daycare. That policy let our employees know that the baby would be okay. It also gave them a little more time to choose a daycare or stay-at-home babysitter. One if the things I discovered was that mothers came to work sooner after giving birth and that they were more comfortable raising their children during that three-month period.

I think that today we are seeing more companies that take family into consideration, something we always tried to do.

Wright

What changed for you that caused you to decide to sell your business?

Fife

I decided to sell my business because I felt that I had taken it as far as I could take it. I had a real high matrix of communication and people. On our letterhead and stamp machine that we used for our office, it said *"working with the best in the business."* That meant our clients were the best in the business and it also meant our employees were the best. What it really meant was all of them were the best in the business. We felt like we worked with the best product manufacturers and national marketing firms in the business.

As the business became more technologically developed, I felt like I had taken the business as far as I could take it. I thought it would be to my advantage to sell to a company that had high tech resources and that the combination of that and the excellent people involved— "the best in the business"—could really take a great team to the next level.

Wright

How has owning/selling your business given rise to your success?

Fife

I sold the business three years ago and the reason I feel successful is because to this day people still contact me to tell me how that business changed their life. I still have clients who call to check in. I did develop personal relationships—friendships—with clients. It is interesting because one of the things that I learned about business is that people really respond to how you care about your business. They will forgive a multitude of problems that are out of your control if they know how much you care and how hard you work.

I think that starting, building, and selling that business added to my success because I now know I can do it. As my children grow older and are graduating college, I can help them start businesses if that is what they choose to do.

I also learned so much about managing people. I am a big believer in the DISC program of personality assessment. I think that being a leader has really helped me to move on. Regarding the term "rising to the top," I am not sure that there is a top because even the "top" has someone to answer to—a board of directors or stockholders, etc. I am not sure that a "top" really exists.

Wright
In rising to the top what are some pitfalls to avoid?

Fife
One of the pitfalls is failure to do individual evaluations at a timely rate. You need to stay on top of people regarding their talents and what they contribute to your organization.

Another thing that I think is a huge pitfall and something that I try to avoid is "putting all your eggs in one basket." Don't think that you have one big client you can work for and that one client can meet all of your financial needs. Thinking this way puts too much responsibility on one client. If something happens to that client the business could experience a financial disaster. Always try to work for diverse clients who can benefit from your expertise ensuring a business plan that can survive losing one of them.

Many times I feel I made a mistake in judgment in allowing clients to extend their payment terms more than ninety days. While our uncollectibles were less than two percent, I still feel I could have been more proactive in keeping accounts receivable current. I suggest making terms shorter—no longer than fifteen days—and staying on top of delinquents.

Wright
What were some of your struggles during your eighteen years of business?

Fife
Some of the struggles included a variable workload. There were times when we had a long-term project we agreed to do or participated in that ended and we didn't have something else to take its place right away. Something would come in at the last minute. Then there were times when the workload was overwhelming. We always had to stay on top of keeping things new and fresh so that we didn't lose good people and we kept moving forward. Anytime one of our

clients was sold there was a real shock wave. That is a huge challenge because mergers happen often, therefore you have to have some way to diversify.

Whenever there was a slow time, one of the things I learned was that if I asked my clients what they needed they would tell me. Always look for things that have added value because if you do have struggles, you are still in the game.

Wright

What are some of the lessons that you walked away with?

Fife

Communication is so important in business whether it is to your own employees or your clients. I strongly believe that communication is the key to a successful business.

Another lesson I learned was to diversify. Don't get tunnel vision about what you are doing in your business. Always look for new opportunities. If something comes to you that you think may be an opportunity, don't take your eye off it because it can lead to something very successful—personally successful and professionally successful.

Wright

How can those lessons help others reading this?

Fife

First of all, I want people to know that I went from being a dental hygienist to being a very successful in-store marketing expert who won national awards and was nationally recognized and if I can do it, they can do it. Others can have hope that their dreams can come true because I did it—I am a model of that. I know you can think of a million reasons why your dreams can't come true, but I want to tell you that I can think of a million and one ways of how they *can* come true. I am living proof of it. I am one of the 5 percent of American women who built a million dollar business. It has provided a foundation for the speaking, consulting, and coaching business I now enjoy.

The decision to be an entrepreneur is one of the best you can make. You will make mistakes but listen to the marketplace and it will tell you what it needs. Then fill the need with value. Oh, one more thing: surround yourself with people like you—only smarter.

Wright

What an interesting conversation. I appreciate the time you've taken in talking with me here and being with us discussing rising to the top.

Fife

Thank you.

Wright

Speaking and writing from her own experience, Bert McCoy Fife made an unexpected 360-degree turn from dental hygienist to in-store marketing entrepreneur. As you have discovered how her rise to the top has a much deeper personal meaning, you may have been inspired to pay attention to signals that it's time for a change for you and to summon your courage and find resources to accomplish your change. You may reach Bert by e-mail at Bert@bertfife.com to make arrangements for her to speak to your business or organization about topics that will help your business and employees grow individually and as a team.

About the Author

BERT MCCOY FIFE graduated from Loyola University, raised five children, and built a successful in-store marketing event company. As one of the 5 percent of American women who have owned a million dollar company, her expertise is in managing and motivating people to achieve their best by utilizing their opportunities and inherent gifts. She currently resides in Baton Rouge, Louisiana, with her Tabby cat. Recently she teamed with Jerie Ford, an award-winning cabaret singer, to perform "Corporate Cabaret" helping businesses and organizations learn and apply behavioral strengths to develop world class people with world class communication skills. Jerie is the singer; Bert's the seminar leader who promises not to sing.

Bert Fife

E-mail: Bert@bertfife.com

Chapter 11

Dr. Madeline Ann Lewis

David Wright (Wright)

Today we're talking with Dr. Madeline Ann Lewis, President and CEO of the Deline Institute for Professional Development. She conducts workshops and seminars specializing in Women's Issues. Dr. Lewis is a passionate believer in self-esteem, desiring to guide women to achieve their best mental, physical, spiritual, and emotional health. Dr. Lewis has provided keynote addresses and workshops for groups such as the National Association of Female Executives (NAFE), Federally Employed Women, the Professional Woman Network, universities, and federal government agencies. Her expertise stems from twenty-one years in the military and twenty years of civilian federal governmental services. She is involved with organizations such as Women Impacting Public Policy and the Professional Woman Speakers Bureau.

Dr. Lewis, welcome to *Rising to the Top: A Guide to Success.*

Dr. Madeline Ann Lewis (Dr. Lewis)

Thank you very much!

Wright

What prompted you to focus on women's career advancement and professional development?

Dr. Lewis

I went into this arena because women bring many wonderful strengths to the workplace in regard to their leadership skills when they are given an equal chance, however, what I have noticed is that most women do not know what their potential may be or what their strengths are. They either do not put themselves in a position to move up the career ladder or they make mistakes that could have been avoided if they only understood what was expected of them once they started climbing the ladder. And, they don't shine their light as bright as they should to let others know they are capable of doing the job.

These were the reasons I wanted to get into this arena. I want to help women to focus on their careers and help them understand some of the things they will need to know in advance and some of the things they can do to advance in their professional careers and personal development.

Wright

What do you feel are the biggest obstacles women face in trying to move up in their careers?

Dr. Lewis

As you know, obstacles will occur in everybody's life when they are trying to reach a goal or they have a vision. It's a wise woman, however, who realizes that adversity can be the catalyst giving her the added strength to achieve her dreams. Unfortunately there's still the gender status belief that continues to create obstacles for women to overcome. Even though studies have shown that women have gained increased access to supervisory and middle-management positions, they still remain under-represented in leadership positions. Women are still more likely to be placed in administrative type positions rather than in an operational position that will let them hold greater responsibility. When they do get into a leadership position, they are more closely scrutinized than their male counterparts.

These are just some of the extra obstacles they have to face—their leadership styles are questioned, their competency is questioned, and they are more closely scrutinized.

Wright

Will you tell our readers what drives you to be so involved with women and their personal and professional development?

Dr. Lewis

I see women all the time who feel that their careers are stagnant. They want to advance, they want to polish their image, and they want to understand the company cultures; however, they do not know what steps they need to take to make these things happen. My goal is to take them to the next step by providing the training and guidance and the confidence for them to be able to think outside the box and to further their progression in the workplace.

At the Deline Institute for Professional Development where I conduct my workshops and seminars, I do one-on-one coaching, and mentoring. I help women see their potential and ultimately help them reach their goals.

Wright

How were you able to figure out what it takes to advance in the workplace?

Dr. Lewis

It took a while, but I did it by taking careful inventory of the women who rose to the top in their professions and learning how they managed to get there. I spent twenty-one years in the military and another twenty years in civilian and federal sectors of the workplace. I've had the opportunity to see how the structure of an organization worked. Most of the organizations were very top-heavy with men, and I took note of how the few women who *did* rise to the top were treated and what was expected of them. I interviewed numerous women who had risen to the top of their professions just to see some of the things it took for them to get there, and the things that it takes for them to stay there.

Now don't get me wrong, not all women face the stereotypes that are heaped upon them because of their leadership styles or maybe questionable competency and things of that nature. Some fare well in organizations and are competent and skilled individuals; but my goal is to help the ones who aren't so fortunate to have the chance to learn what they need to do to advance in the workplace while gaining the credibility they deserve.

Wright

What do you feel women need to possess to move into leadership roles?

Dr. Lewis

Women definitely need to possess the skills required for the position. They need to be competent, and it's very important that they have confidence and impeccable credentials. I also feel they need to possess a high self-esteem.

Another important trait that they should possess is the ability to listen. Good listeners listen with their ears *and* their mind. Each one needs good communication skills and she should be a visionary. Every good leader I've ever seen has a vision. Leadership is about setting a vision or new direction. Good leaders can probably close their eyes and picture the entire concept in their mind. They need to possess self-control. They need to be able to inspire others. They need to know when to pick their battles. And finally, they need to possess good common sense.

Wright

What advice would you give to women who aspire to move up the career ladder into leadership positions?

Dr. Lewis

There is a lot of advice I could put out there for women who want to climb the career ladder. Some of the points I consider to be the most important include:

1. Be a strong role model!
2. Be consistent with others no matter who they are or what they know.
3. Don't pre-judge—listen closely to what others have to say.
4. Use criticism as a tool for self-improvement. Take criticism for what it is, and move on.
5. Learn to speak the language of management within the organization where you are trying to move up the career ladder.
6. Accept the fact that you cannot please everyone. Trust me, it's just not going to happen.
7. If you can't both be liked *and* respected, then I think you should be sure that you are respected.
8. And remember, first impressions are very important.

Wright

Who are some of the people who influenced your life and caused you to focus on this area of expertise?

Dr. Lewis

The person who had the major influence on me in my life was my mother, Mrs. Lilly Lewis. She was a firm believer that you always share your knowledge with those who need help or guidance. She also believed that when you get to the top you should pull someone up with you. These are some of the reasons why I do what I do and why I'm in the area of personal and professional development and career advancement for women. Now, I realize that my mom was not differentiating between helping men or women, but in most cases women need more help in career advancement. Men will usually help each other out.

Wright

How did you begin putting together workshops and seminars to guide women in their personal and professional development?

Dr. Lewis

I started the Deline Institute for Professional Development for women to have a formal environment where they are able to share their thoughts, their joys, their weaknesses, and in some cases share their success. The workshops and seminars I offer are: Leadership Skills for Women, Overcoming Being All Things to All People, Mirror! Mirror!, Taking Stress Inventory, The Image of a Female Leader, and First Impressions: Issues Impacting Women. These are just a few topics that are covered at the institute for women that can help them to accomplish their goals and hopefully take them into a more healthy life, emotionally, mentally, spiritually, and physically.

I put together the workshops because I think they really deal with life issues and guide women, making them take a good look at themselves as well as some of the things that may be going on in life that most of us can definitely relate to. I think the seminars also provide ways to make adjustments in behavior, attitude, image that might be necessary.

Wright

Would you recommend this area of involvement to other women?

Dr. Lewis

Definitely, yes, I certainly would recommend more women get involved in career and professional development and mentoring and coaching. The reason why is not that they would be giving themselves a label of being a "know-it-all," but actually, I believe women would do a lot of good for many people who would definitely appreciate it! Just think about how good you feel when you're able to give someone advice and help him or her and know that you were the one who was instrumental in that person's career advancement, professional development, or in helping build self-esteem or confidence. It has been said that "knowledge is power," but I say sharing knowledge is empowering.

Wright

So how did you come up with the topics you use in your workshops?

Dr. Lewis

I think the topics just cover life and everyday issues as they relate to women. I want women to be able to expand their awareness. I want women to know it's okay to be good to themselves. I want women to transform their challenges into successes. I want women to eliminate their barriers and I want women to know that they are precious and that they can accomplish anything that they set out to accomplish. All it takes is persistence, discipline, and focus! Sometimes you have to bring these things to the forefront because sometimes it takes that extra jolt to become aware of them.

The workshops that I provide and the topics that I speak on give women that reality where they can realize, "Yeah, I see how that relates to me!" or, "Yeah, I'm doing that and I really need to correct that" or maybe, "That's something I need to incorporate so I can advance in my career!"

That's why I picked the topics I use.

Wright

Most of the things you've talked about here today would also be good advice for men. Did you ever think about branching out and including more people?

Dr. Lewis

I have had men attend my seminars, and most of the seminars I teach men can and should attend. I certainly don't bar them from attending. In the workplace, there are things that happen to women that men may not be totally aware of or they may not be aware of how they affect women. So, definitely, I think that my seminars and workshops would be good for men too!

Also, the workshops can be tailored for any audience, so that's one of the things people will notice on my Web site: www.delineinstitute.net. I indicate that a particular workshop or seminar can be tailored for any client's specific needs. My seminars and workshops are meant to motivate, inspire, and elevate lives through education. I am sure men would benefit.

Wright

So what is the one thing that you would like to leave with women as it relates to their professional development?

Dr. Lewis

Never, ever let anyone make you second-guess yourself or your skills. If you know that you have the credentials and the talent and the skills to be in a certain position, and you know that you can *do* that job—then do it! Do it well and do it with confidence. In the words of Les Brown, "Shoot for the moon! Even if you miss, you'll still be among the stars!"

Wright

This has been a great conversation and I really appreciate your taking this time this morning to talk about this really important issue of women, especially the fact that they have feelings—particularly about their potential in the workplace. Men don't talk much about feelings today, and I appreciate your insight. I've learned a lot, and I'm sure our readers will too.

Dr. Lewis

I hope so, I really hope they do! Thank you.

About the Author

DR. MADELINE ANN LEWIS is President/CEO of the Deline Institute for Professional Development. She conducts workshops and seminars specializing in women's issues. Dr. Lewis is a passionate believer in self-esteem, desiring to guide women to achieve their best mental, physical, spiritual, and emotional health. Dr. Lewis has provided keynote addresses, workshops, and seminars for groups such as the Federally Employed Women, Professional Woman Network, universities, and federal government agencies. Her expertise stems from twenty-one years in the military and twenty years of civilian federal government service. She is involved with organizations such as the National Association of Female Executives, Women Impacting Public Policy, and the Professional Woman Speakers Bureau. She was also nominated for the Office Depot 2007 Business Woman of the Year Award.

Dr. Madeline Ann Lewis
Deline Institute for Professional Development
P.O. Box 5091
Capital Heights, MD 20891-5091
E-mail: sioc@aol.com
www.delineinstitute.net
www.protrain.net/lewis.htm

Chapter 12

DR. EDWARD P. FISZER

David Wright (Wright)
Today we're talking with Edward P. Fiszer. Dr. Fiszer's mission is to ensure a copy of *Daily Positives: Inspiring Greatness in the Next Generation* is placed in the hands of every child enrolled in a school in North and South America in English or Spanish.

Dr. Fiszer, welcome to *Rising to the Top: A Guide to Success.*

Dr. Edward Fiszer (Fiszer) (pronounced "Fisher")
Thank you so much. It is a pleasure to be here.

Wright
Why did you write *Daily Positives: Inspiring Greatness in the Next Generation?*

Fiszer
The determining factor in the future success of any child comes from the modeling of a positive attitude and relentless tenacity

learned from family members. Yet families are often too busy to have discussions of future goals unless it is part of their daily routine.

Daily Positives is a tool families and educators can use to ensure that young people are fed inspirational "mental protein" on a daily basis rather than solely having their perceptions of how they should think, speak, and act molded by their peers and the media.

Aristotle said, "We are what we repeatedly do. Excellence, then, is not an act but a habit." Our habits are our success.

Just as a big project necessitates the visualization of outcomes and determination of next actions that must be taken, the future of every child must be treated in the same manner. Daily life is filled with learning opportunities and lessons children need to take in. The fact that family members are overscheduled, stressed out, and tired does not mean important life lessons must then not be discussed.

Family mealtimes or a before bedtime ritual of reading *Daily Positives* or other inspirational material will solve this gap that exists in too many households in this country. In less than five minutes, material can be read and then discussed. Inspirational material naturally leads to discussion of what future goals lay ahead of each family member and what he or she needs to do to reach these goals.

Adults as well as children absolutely need reminders and encouragement in areas of tenacity, responsibility, and other character traits. The most valuable lesson a child can learn ultimately is to never give up on his or her goals and dreams. Too many negative messages in the media show unsuccessful people who inadvertently serve as models for others because the message of their mistakes and failures are noted by those listening. Instead, positive examples should be repeatedly shared since every individual becomes what he or she thinks about, and thoughts tend to be shaped by the messages taken in from the environment. For this reason, those involved in the lives of children have the responsibility to expose young people to relentlessly positive messages, stories, and experiences.

Wright

History does show that by exposing people to what works, they will follow in the footsteps of the successful, whereas the sharing of negative information tends to lead to negative behavior.

Fiszer

One of my favorite Stephen Covey concepts is that every individual and organization is perfectly aligned to receive their current results. Results don't lie. If you are not getting the results you want, there is something you are doing or some aspect of your life that is out of alignment.

If you show people what they should aspire to be through the modeling provided by successful people in the past, they will align their thinking with the successful models. Many young people do not have exposure to positive role models and are entitled to some source of encouragement.

As the principal of an elementary school, I wanted positive thinking and the idea of success as contingent on effort and good choices to permeate the school environment. Using the school's sound system, every morning from the first day I began working at Pinetree Community School in Santa Clarita, California, I started the morning announcements with an inspirational message that included an introduction to a quote and an application piece. Every day I would take an inspirational quote that meant a lot to me and created a message that would be heard by students in kindergarten through sixth grade. This was my "homework" because I had to have it ready for each morning's announcements.

The response was tremendous. Another reason it came about is that I am a firm believer in taking whatever projects one is working on and consider multiple uses of that work to help as many people as possible with the initial effort.

Daily Positives is valuable for families as well as educators because once you develop the ritual of giving positive information to young people each day, it is something they begin to rely on.

Just as anyone who gardens understands, if one cultivates a garden regularly, the results are easily attained and the ritual of gardening becomes more fulfilling as the results multiply. Often gardeners are complemented for their results. Yet the secret of their success lies in their daily routine. The gardener who works each day makes a huge difference over time as opposed to the person who tries to cram in a lot of gardening once or twice a year while dealing with an overwhelming task that could never be compared to the energizing ritual of gardening. Similarly, an individual cannot go the gym once a month to stay healthy. Success lies in one's daily routine.

How crucial it is then for parents and caretakers of children to incorporate a daily time to tend to the garden that lies within the mind of a child. Leaving the child's mind to itself will produce weeds. The minds of young people absolutely must be nourished regularly rather than tended to after negative consequences are visible.

I know firsthand of the power of these messages because the quotes themselves have helped inspire me to stay focused on the positive outcomes I desire.

Wright

Why are you targeting continents rather than solely the United States?

Fiszer

I've been influenced by great authors who emphasize the idea of "big hairy audacious goals," such as Stephen Covey, Tom Peters, Jim Collins and others. If you are going to aspire to do something wonderful, think big and see how you can set your work in motion to do the most good for the most people. Having *Daily Positives* available in Spanish as well as English can realize measurable outcomes across several continents. It corresponds nicely with the quote from Goethe, "Dream no small dreams for they have no power to move men."

Each page in the book contains an inspirational quote, an introduction (perhaps giving the background of the author), and then an application piece where it talks about how these young children have the power to positively impact the environment. They can imitate the thinking of the person quoted and through their thoughts and actions can create a wonderful environment in their family or in their school.

The writings of Stephen Covey also exposed me to the notion of a space existing between the time of a stimulus and an individual's conscious choice. Someone can use that space in time to show he or she is responsible or able to control his or her response. *Daily Positives* is a wonderful tool to emphasize the notion that people have the power to choose—they are not powerless despite some very, very difficult circumstances.

Wright

Tell me about how you have used *Daily Positives* to help organizations fundraise for their own causes.

Fiszer

As this book was created I really felt that it should be used to help other organizations that are doing powerful things to impact the world in a good way. Since fundraising is a key issue for nonprofit and service organizations, the use of this book as a fundraising tool would create a win-win situation for all involved—the book reaches like-minded families while allowing money to flow toward a worthy cause.

Personally, I detest the demeaning fundraising that organizations are left to use such as overpriced, low quality wrapping paper and chocolate that people don't need and don't want. Instead, why not offer something families can use?

Wright

What success have you experienced so far with *Daily Positives?*

Fiszer

I've had quite a few unique comments from different people that indicate the quality of response received so far. There are adult staff members at schools where I have used *Daily Positives* who, upon hearing the morning announcements, have shared that they feel as though I am speaking directly to them, and that impacts their attitude on a regular basis. It helps them refocus on what is most important. After being absent, students would ask, "What was the morning message?" Parents have shared that kindergarten age students were using words like, "persevere." They would tell the parent, "I persevered today because Dr. Fiszer said you need to persevere when you're trying to do something good when you don't want to." And, "I persevered when I was eating my vegetables in the cafeteria."

In addition, with my charter school, NEW Academy Canoga Park, I was able to provide a copy of the book for each student enrolled at the school during the first year of operation. Many of them told me unique things such as, "I read half of your book to my little brother last night and we really, really like it." Parents who have come to the United States from other countries have stated that *Daily Positives* has helped them learn English because they would read it every night with their children.

My experience with giving copies to a large group of children reminded me that not all children have personal copies of books at home. Schools are in the business of lending books to children but not necessarily supplying personal copies for ongoing use at home. Often, families whose money is focused on food and shelter have little access to books.

The material is accessible to all school-age children. Children can read it on their own. Adults have told me that they read it themselves. I've had one individual, whose child lives a three-hour drive away, tell me that he uses it on the phone with his son every day.

Discussing the inspirational quotes brings him closer to his child and then the discussion naturally leads to a conversation about what the goals are for each of them and what challenges they have faced.

I see it as doing a lot of good for a lot of people and certainly this is something that corporations and larger organizations could consider giving as a gift to employees for perhaps Mother's Day or Father's Day or graduation time in the months of May and June. It is something that is very useful.

One book critic in her review said, "I receive so many books but this is one that I am definitely keeping."

Wright

Do you have any favorite passages from *Daily Positives?*

Fiszer

I do. I really feel strongly about the first passage with a little known quote by a man named Gilbert Arland and the quote is: "When an archer misses the mark he turns and looks for the fault within himself. Failure to hit the bull's eye is never the fault of the target or the bow. To improve your aim, improve yourself."

The blame for failure is within the person and the choices the person made, the skill level, or the timing of the event. Just like a student who wants to be a better athlete or a better reader or a better friend he or she needs to identify the barriers to success and put in the time with effort and practice to help skills develop over time.

One of the books my current staff read during the 2006–2007 school year was *The Power of Full Engagement.* This book emphasizes that energy rather than time needs to be managed to truly enhance productivity. The book highlights how the most successful people maintain rituals that keep them in alignment with their goals, limits distractions, and enhances their energy. These rituals include spending time with those most important to them, taking periodic breaks, eating healthy foods, exercising, and keeping workspaces organized.

Similarly, energy will be enhanced among family members who use mealtimes or bedtime rituals to share inspirational information. The conversations that arise from these activities are among the most influential in a young person's life as well as in the life of the adult. Robert Maxson, then president of California State University Long Beach, once visited my UCLA cohort during my doctoral program and said, "Energy comes from happiness." Families will feel increased energy nurturing young people because there truly is not a better use of time and alignment toward exciting goals.

Some families have expressed that mealtimes can sometimes be very stressful because people often routinely share problems and complaints rather than their goals or the positive things that have happened during the day.

Wright

What books have inspired you?

Fiszer

Key books that have inspired me include: Stephen Covey's *The 7 Habits of Highly Effective People,* Jack Canfield's *The Success Principles,* and the works of Shakespeare.

Other books I use when speaking to organizations include Eric Jensen's work in his book, *Teaching with the Brain in Mind,* where he discusses incredible ramifications for teachers, such as how anxiety and poor health habits impact student learning negatively. The brain chemicals do not function at a level that is appropriate for learning if the morning has been excessively stressful or there is relentlessly difficult problems and yelling in the home and a negative atmosphere. Where there's a positive atmosphere, the brain is most like a sponge.

Another author I really think highly of is Dr. Csikszentmihalyi whose research is all about a state called "flow." This is a state where an individual is deeply immersed in the work at hand and time passes quickly and effortlessly. Examples of times when people might experience flow include reading a book, writing, or putting a puzzle together. The connections between his research and organizations are incredibly pertinent since employees immersed in what they are doing are prone to enjoy their work and have creative breakthroughs.

Wright

How would you compare *Daily Positives* to those books?

Fiszer

There is clearly a connection regarding positive choices. Stephen Covey states in *The 7 Habits of Highly Effective People,* "Your personal victories are what drive your public victories." Without private victories where you are proactively choosing to do what is most important to you and are fulfilling a vision, you can't really be as successful and as helpful to others. Those private victories stem from your thinking. This brings to mind that quote from Albert Einstein when the reporter asked him, "What is the most important question facing humanity today?"

Einstein replied, "I think the most important question facing humanity is, 'is the universe a friendly place?'"

If you are confident that the universe is friendly in that others are there to help you and that your dreams can become reality, then you are right—you can accomplish these things. However, if you feel the universe is unfriendly, you are absolutely correct as well in that you will not accomplish incredible things and no one will have an interest in helping you.

Daily Positives is aligned with that type of thinking because it states over and over that you need to be responsible for your thoughts, words, and actions. Challenges and setbacks are a natural part of growth. They are successfully dealt with by a positive mindset.

Wright

You are the founding principal of an independent charter school in Los Angeles called NEW Academy Canoga Park (NACP). How is NACP different from traditional public schools?

Fiszer

As the founding principal of a brand new elementary charter school I had the pleasure of hiring all employees. Those employees helped determine the mission statement and the core values—the direction in which we would head and how we would arrive there. Intense collaboration was present from the start. We discussed how we didn't necessarily need "school rules" like *don't run* and *don't yell.* Rather, the core values were designed to be the aspirations all students, staff, and families would strive to model through their daily actions. Our four core values are:

1. Children learn in different ways on different days.
2. Everyone is deserving of the highest respect.
3. Doing extra makes a difference.
4. Everyone is responsible for individual choices.

The core values are on the walls of every classroom, in daily conversation among staff and students, on the back of the business cards of staff members, and in the school literature. These guiding principles set a high standard for all stakeholders from day one. Students who make mistakes are simply asked which core value they were not modeling and the discussion leads them to realign their thoughts, words, and actions with the school's expectations.

The collaborative culture was formed from the first time teachers gathered together. The school property was under construction until the final days prior to the opening. For that reason we met during the prior months in unique locations. Prior to our first meeting we read *The Art of Possibility* and *The 7 Habits of Highly Effective People*, using the key concepts as a common language among staff members as the mission and core values were developed. We hiked in the Santa Monica Mountains, attended a concert at the Hollywood Bowl, and attended a yoga class together.

Likewise, trust among parents was well established prior to the opening of the school. Parent meetings were conducted where questions were answered, teachers were met, and parents were involved in decisions such as uniform colors.

Wright

What grades are you talking about?

Fiszer

We serve kindergarten through fifth grade students.

Wright

How was NEW Academy Canoga Park influenced by your first book, *How Teachers Learn Best: An Ongoing Professional Development Model?*

Fiszer

Collaboration is too often missing from typical schools. My research shows that schools incorporating an ongoing professional development model focused on improving student achievement according to collaboratively established goals are more responsive to student needs and maintain a high level of trust, which directly corresponds to morale. These schools tend to prioritize professional dialogue, ensuring regular time is set aside for teacher collaboration both within and between grade levels, and peer observation.

I think it's rare for teachers to observe one another in practice because it does cost the school money to pay for a substitute teacher or someone else who would supervise the children. Yet it's clearly a powerful learning tool that has high impact. The observing teacher will note teaching strategies used, management routines, and other details he or she would not be in a position to notice if that teacher was in that classroom at any other time. The observer takes his or her own notes and the observations are of a non-evaluative nature. Peer observation tends to go a longer way than some of the professional development sessions I've attended where people are not fully committed to taking the information and applying it.

Other examples of the collaborative culture include having a form of Lesson Study which involves a grade level being released for two full days of collaboration in which they create a series of lessons together, present those lessons, and dialogue about what was successful and what could be improved. Teachers collaboratively develop a lesson and go into one classroom, a teacher presents it, and the other teachers take notes about what worked and what did not work. They all hope for success since they are each invested in the process. After the lesson is presented they discuss details, refine the presentation, and either have another person present the same lesson or use the feedback gathered by the observers to rework the next lesson in the unit of lessons planned, while a different teacher presents.

Watching each other in practice allows details to be compared related to the smallest details of teaching, including how resources are literally distributed in the classroom and management techniques. It builds morale.

NEW Academy Canoga Park teachers write grants to fund additional classroom supplies because they recognize that if they have a good idea, lack of funding from the government should not stop them from providing exemplary experiences for their students. These teachers proactively take initiative and recognize that every choice they make impacts their environment. In fact, teachers who successfully contact businesses and organizations to receive support motivate others to do the same. The excitement is contagious. This is the exact opposite of many schools where the atmosphere is toxically reactive with negativity focused on everything teachers do not have or are not given. It's a collaborative method and I think NEW Academy Canoga Park is exemplary regarding this form of ongoing professional development.

Every teacher has business cards. They are used to build relationships with community members, in local stores, or in any other situation that can, in effect, advertise the school. These actions have directly influenced the positive word-of-mouth influence our school has in the community.

Many campuses do not have openness toward visitors. NEW Academy Canoga Park loves having visitors tour classrooms to see what we do, how we do it, and what other bridges can be built to make the school stronger. Reaching out to local organizations builds a bond between the school and the community. The community knows our students, the Dolphins, are educated to align their thoughts, words, and actions with excellent core values and this enhances their value as citizens of the community.

We also have an Alumni Association and we invite our former students to return twice each year. The students look for their names on the banner in the back of the gymnasium where their names are listed along with their chosen profession. At alumni meetings they share if their careers are on track. They know they will always be Dolphins and will always be welcome. It's a true win/win situation.

Other areas where I feel NEW Academy Canoga Park shines include regularly presenting at the annual California Association of Charter Schools Conference.

We also do something I think few schools do in that we have "Fun Meetings." Rather than sitting together for a few hours of announcements from the principal, we go to a museum or do an activity together such as a self-defense class or painting pottery. These practices foster morale and remind people that self-actualization ultimately happens when you blur the lines between work and play. You cannot work all the time and be absolutely successful. You need to release stress through enjoyable activities that essentially help bring about a state of "flow." When you look forward to being with the people you work with while doing unique, innovative things, joy is felt and that ultimately transmits to the students and families who are our primary customers.

Wright

What key concepts do you emphasize when speaking to school groups and non-educational groups?

Fiszer

Trust is the key factor directly related to success in every organization. *The Leadership Challenge* and many other management texts bear out that without trust, the work of individuals and groups becomes sluggish at best and irrelevant at worst. Results are not present without trust. As common sense as that is, most organizations would directly benefit from sessions directly related to this issue and related to discussions on fostering a collaborative culture.

This is also true in education. Teachers cannot collaborate if trust does not exist. Teachers learn best when they are able to openly collaborate, practice new innovations, and compare results. Essentially, there needs to be respect in the air in that it is clear that every teacher is a professional who has something to offer. This corresponds to the maintenance of high expectations and accountability at the school site.

This crucial ongoing professional development model is presented to schools and organizations with fantastic results. It is a cost effective way to spend development dollars. In addition, the success literature offers a huge amount of information organizations can learn from. Ultimately every organization needs employees to foster an environment where people are in a state of "flow" because they are accountable for results in clearly defined areas where they understand how to apply their strengths to assigned tasks.

For parent groups I work with, I use these concepts as well as the work of authors like Dr. Daniel J. Siegel, who wrote *Parenting from the Inside Out.* There he talks about the notion of a cohesive narrative where parents need to fully recognize that they're teaching their children through their example and through their stories every day. Children learn to overcome obstacles by knowing what the family has gone through. Stories are universal. They are found in every human culture. They involve logical sequencing of events. They help regulate our emotions because emotions and analytical thinking are intertwined.

There's a huge audience that would benefit from hearing about the need for consistent messages from parents about the difficulties they have gone through as well as about their successes. How did they ultimately become successful? How did they have something similar happen to them yet they still persevered and felt good about the results? Helping parents refine their own stories and turning things that happen in a child's life into reminders of the greatness to come, I think represents staggering benefits to children.

For this reason I developed a Web site and online newsletter found at www.responsiveparent.com. It is crucial that parents receive periodic reminders and ideas regarding how they can provide a stimulating, healthy environment for their children. The mission of www.responsiveparent.com is to provide information and resources to forward thinking parents who realize current actions generate future results. It follows the spirit of Aristotle's words: "We are what we repeatedly do. Excellence, then, is not an act but a habit."

Wright

If every child in North and South America who was given a copy of *Daily Positives* received a message from you, what would it be?

Fiszer

The message is tenacity. If individuals never give up and relentlessly pursue helping others through great dreams they will create a better world. Our thoughts, words, and actions have impact far beyond our family circle. Within the family, what is the family doing to make a positive impact on the neighborhood? Regarding the child in the school setting, how is the child impacting the classroom? How is the classroom impacting the entire school? Are the individuals in school as a group impacting the entire community?

Ultimately, if tenacity is fostered among children, they will understand how they have great impact, just as a stone thrown into a pond—the ripples in the water impact all levels of the pond. I think that's the most powerful message they can receive.

Wright

Well, what a great conversation, Dr. Fiszer. I really appreciate your taking all this time with me to answer these questions. It sounds like you have some very impressive projects underway.

Fiszer

Thank you so much; it was a real pleasure to talk with you.

Wright

Today we've been talking with Edward P. Fiszer, EdD. We've been talking about his book, *Daily Positives: Inspiring Greatness in the Next Generation,* and how he uniquely reads passages to his students every morning using spaced repetition, of the greatest learning models to form new personalities and to feed new minds. I think he knows what he's talking about. I'm going to go out and get this book now just because of this conversation.

Dr. Fiszer, thank you so much for being with us today on *Rising to the Top: A Guide to Success.*

About The Author

DR. EDWARD FISZER speaks and consults with organizations on leadership, collaboration, and teacher professional development. Born and raised in Los Angeles, California, Dr. Fiszer received his Bachelor of Arts degree in History at UCLA and multiple-subject teaching credential at California State University, Northridge. While serving as an elementary school teacher and English language development specialist in Burbank, he attended the Educational Leadership Academy at Pepperdine University for a Master of Science degree in Education Administration. He returned to UCLA for a doctorate through the Educational Leadership Program, while working as a site administrator. For four years he served as a principal in Santa Clarita. In 2005 Dr. Fiszer became the founding principal of NEW Academy Canoga Park, an elementary charter school which emphasizes art and science, as well as character development. This innovative school is known for the affordable housing development directly adjacent to the school created by New Economics for Women. Dr. Fiszer and NEW Academy Canoga Park teachers created four core values when the school opened to which all staff, students, and families aspire:

1. Children learn in different ways on different days
2. Everyone is deserving of the highest respect
3. Doing extra makes a difference
4. Everyone is responsible for individual choices.

Dr. Fiszer reads motivational messages over the sound system each day to emphasize tenacity, responsibility, and other character traits. Dr. Fiszer compiled his inspirational messages into his third book, *Daily Positives: Inspiring Greatness in the Next Generation. Daily Positives* and the practice of reading inspirational passages to students have been recognized as a Promising Practice by the Character Education Partnership. Dr. Fiszer was recognized as a "Champion of Children" in April 2007 during the Week of the Young Child by the Los Angeles City Council. Dr. Fiszer's other books include: *How Teachers Learn Best: An Ongoing Professional Development Model* and *Thoughts to Inspire: Daily Messages for Young People.*

Dr. Edward Fiszer
Fiszer Concepts, LLC
26873 Sierra Highway
Santa Clarita, CA 91321
Phone: 661.255.2018
E-mail: efiszer@fiszerconcepts.com
www.dailypositives.com
NEW Academy Canoga Park: www.nacpdolphins.org

Chapter 13

PATRICIA BALL, CSP, CPAE

David E. Wright (Wright)

Patricia is a CSP and CPAE. She is president of Corporation Communications. She served as president of the National Speakers Association and served as International President of the International Federation for Professional Speakers. Patricia is a Certified Speaking Professional, communication specialist, a keynoter, diversity trainer, author, and presentation skills coach. A graduate of Washington University, she has been on the lecture platform since 1972, speaking nationally and internationally. Patricia has helped thousands of executives, salespeople, and others achieve greater success in their personal and professional lives through the dramatic impact of her workshops and lectures. In 1994, she was inducted into the Council of Peers Award for Excellence Hall of Fame, the Oscar of the speaking profession. Less than 120 people worldwide have received this honor, and only twenty-five women have received this award. Patricia has received intensive training in diversity and gender issues from the Copeland Griggs Institute in California.

Patricia Ball, welcome to *Rising to the Top: A Guide to Success.*

Patricia Ball (Ball)
Thank you. It's great to be here.

Wright
Patricia, your credentials are incredible. Will you tell our readers a little bit about your background and how you chose the speaking and training industry?

Ball
The speaking and training industry actually chose me. I began as a dance instructor, many years ago. I had my own dance studio at age sixteen—my first leadership role—and had fourteen years of dance training by then.

I ran the dance studio for three years, two of which were during my first two years of college at Washington University. Then, while in college, and thereafter, I studied communications, speech, and theater.

After college I became a professional actor doing commercials and one-woman shows and plays. About ten years after doing all of that, I put together a series of one-woman shows, because I felt it was very important to be able to control my own destiny. In a sense, I was doing my own casting instead of waiting for the phone to ring.

In 1972, I was selected to be in a speakers' showcase, even though what I did at that time was acting. I took some pieces from my theatrical one-woman shows and showcased them. A meeting planner came up afterwards and was very complimentary. He said I was talented and he enjoyed the showcase. He would like for me to speak to his employees, but they were interested in not only entertainment. They wanted to know what I could do to help them learn. Of course, I do have a degree in communications and theater and speech, so I told him that I could put together a communications program for his company. He was excited about that. I was equally excited because I could see the vision and the new direction toward which that was leading me. This is how my speaking and training career began, and I have been at it ever since.

Wright
And doing it very well, I might add.

Ball
Thank you very much.

Wright

I've watched your successful career for many years. You've trained leadership groups and you've led your own company. Looking at leadership issues from both sides, what do most executives struggle with in their quest for becoming better leaders?

Ball

Really, it boils down to the field in which I teach—communications. It boils down to the executive making an appropriate connection with people. Many executives I've been in contact with lack a strong dose of empathy. They do everything they think is right, but they lack that connective tissue, that ability to put themselves in the other person's shoes, to read between the lines, read what's not being said. So to me, one of the most important attributes of the leader is empathy and good communication skills, understanding executive communications between the leader and his or her employees.

Wright

The focus of your presentations seems to be communications. Since great leaders say that communication is such a vital part of leadership, how would you suggest people in leadership positions hone their communication skills?

Ball

First of all, I'm a strong believer in hands-on training, reading communications books, attending seminars, and getting private coaching if necessary. I am a presentation skills coach and I firmly believe that being able to present effectively is necessary for executives.

Then, after studying, you need to practice it. You need to think about your audience members, who, in the case of the leader, are the customers and employees with whom they come in contact. If you can figure out the customers' needs and wants, if you understand the needs and wants of your organization, and if you can mesh those together, you will be a very effective leader.

Leaders need to learn the skills of listening. Listening is one of the most important skills. A lot of leaders know how to speak well, but they don't know how to listen well. They need to learn how to use silence. They know how to put words together, but silence is a wonderful technique. Being silent allows you to hear what the other person has to say. People are afraid of silence, so they will rush in to fill in the space, which in turn, gives you additional information. You need to be able to read non-verbal clues, or what the other person is saying that he or she may not be putting into words. You need to be sensitive to the needs of other people. You need to be a good questioner as well as a good listener.

You certainly need to be knowledgeable about your field, your products, your services, and people in general. A lot of skills are necessary there.

Wright

Someone told me recently that the end result of most communication is misunderstanding. When I asked him why, he said that people don't communicate anymore. They just take turns talking.

Ball

My daughter once said something that was profound. (Of course, we all have profound daughters and sons sometimes, don't we?) But she said, "What did you say, Mom? I didn't hear you because I had my answer running." Isn't that true of so many of us?

Wright

I've done that before.

Ball

Truly, we're thinking about what we're going to say next, and therefore, we don't hear what has been said to us. Effective listening is *re*acting to what's going on around you and to what the other person has said.

Wright

You're the author of *Straight Talk Is More than Words, Persuasive Communications: The Key to Achieving Your Goals*. Would you tell our readers a little bit about the book, and why you wrote it?

Ball

I'll answer the second part of that question first, if I may. I wrote the book because I have a fascination with straight talk. In my opinion, *straight* talk means *power communications*. "Power" is a fascinating word. It has both negative meanings and positive meanings. It can mean manipulation and control, which are two of the negative definitions we think of when we think of power.

In my book, I only use it in a positive way. I tried to think of all the ways in which it's important for us to communicate effectively with other people, or be a straight talker. The premise of the book is based on an analogy of a play. I start out with the Shakespeare quote, "All the world's a stage. All the men and women are merely players. They have their exits and entrances, and one man in his time plays many parts," I believe that's true. I think that we are continually playing a part. We are a different person as a leader than we are perhaps in our personal life and we are different with our children than we are with our friends. Many of the same traits may still be there. When I say playing a role, I don't mean acting—I mean using some of the communication skills.

The first thing I explore in the book is understanding yourself. This gets into some inner or internal tools of power—some inner kinds of strength. Then, I discuss some external tools of power and that looks at necessary verbal skills, non-verbal skills, behavioral skills, and understanding the other gender. That's certainly an important tool in today's world.

I also look at conflict situations, understanding meetings, how to get the most out of meetings, and how to be more persuasive in meetings. I have four chapters (that's a lot of chapters) on speaking skills, because I believe it's such an important business skill. Not only does public speaking give you exposure, but it also gives you the confidence that carries over into other areas of your life.

And then the final couple of chapters have to do with image and dress or what I call the dress rehearsal, which is putting it all together and making it work for you.

Wright

In your book, you write about the problem of misunderstandings between genders. If you were advising the leader of a company or an organization, how would you suggest this problem be addressed to ensure better communication between men and women?

Ball

It's important to understand that men and women are indeed different from each other. For a long time we tried to pretend we were all the same, and it didn't matter as long as you treated everybody the same. That approach simply doesn't work in today's world. A good leader will learn to recognize and respect the other gender's style because there are communication style differences.

In a sense, the leader needs to become an androgynous manager. He or she should use the strength that works best in any given situation. For example, if you're a woman dealing with a man, speaking of verbal skills, men are often better at statistics. They are more interested in succinct, direct talk that cuts to the chase. Knowing that is the preferred communication style of men, if you adapt that style when you're dealing with them you'll be more effective. It doesn't mean you become a man. All it means is that you will be using what works best in the given situation. You might end up using a traditionally female style in one situation and a traditionally male style in another situation.

Wright

Sometimes my wife comes in and says things like, "Guess who I saw today?" And I'll say, "Who did you see?" And she says, "Well, I was walking down the hall there at the mall, and I was wearing my red dress . . . " And I'm thinking, "Get to the point!"

Ball

Women often do waffle or elaborate about the point. Many women don't get directly to it. This is where we need to be very careful. You can't stereotype and you can't generalize. When I say women do this and men do this, I certainly don't mean all women or all men. There are many exceptions across the board. But patterns of behavior do exist. If we can learn to recognize those patterns, it can be beneficial.

Wright

That is right. You know, many people use the terms "management" and "leadership" interchangeably. Do you think there's a difference between the two? If so, would you point out some of the differences for us?

Ball

I believe there's a very strong difference. Years ago, I read an article from *The Harvard Business Review* by a professor from Harvard. He felt that the two words were not interchangeable. I don't necessarily agree. If business managers fail to consider the importance of leadership dynamics, then all they end up doing is managing "things" and people, but they will not be taking the group anywhere. Managers need more leadership skills than management skills. You can hire a manager, but you need leadership skills.

I think the most important trait that differentiates leaders from managers is vision. Leaders have long-range goals and vision, and they know how to empower others to follow that vision and those goals. Managers have the job of putting all the resources at hand—people and materials, etc.—together to achieve those long-range goals and develop a system that will help achieve them. Another example is managers often manage things. Leaders manage people.

Wright

Patricia, you have written extensively about diversity in the work place. A few years ago, diversity meant black and white. Today every conceivable culture is a part of America's workforce. I would think that leaders would need to understand diversity issues. So, where do they go to get this information?

Ball

I have a number of books in my library, and I pulled a few that I thought would be good sources for the person beginning to be extremely interested in diversity. One is called, *Beyond Race and Gender* and it's by R. Roosevelt Thomas. It's an excellent book. There's another called *Bridging Cultural Barriers for Corporate Success,* by Saundra Thiederman, PhD. Another example is, *The Diversity Advantage,* by Lenora Billings-Harris. And finally, Catherine Fyock has written a book called, *America's Workforce Is Coming of Age.* This one has to do with the aging workforce in America, but it's also very interesting and relevant. Any of these would be an excellent start for anyone who doesn't have a beginning knowledge of diversity.

I think what's more important than what diversity is, is what it is not. You pointed out one of the most important factors. People sometimes think of diversity as being a black and white issue or a race and gender issue. It is not that. It is about respecting all differences and that can mean age, physical disabilities, flex time, lifestyle related concerns, and sexual orientation.

It's not about the exclusion of white males, which is another misconception. It used to be in the workplace that the white male was expected to understand and respect everybody else, but when you think about it, the white male is part of that diversity. Certainly a fifty-five-year-old white male manager, for example, has different needs and wants than a thirty-year-old white male manager. You need to understand and respect those differences and be able to deal with them.

It's really about creating a culture that enables all employees to contribute their full potential. It's not about focusing on differences of groups. It *is* about a diversity of ideas and human potential. Here's a definition that works for me: diversity is the full utilization of all human resource potential.

Wright

That is great.

Ball

There's an outdated approach that no longer works, and people are still using this approach. It used to be years and years ago, that managers felt people needed to be assimilated into the workplace into the mainstream. Everyone needed to be like everybody else. That was the era when women looked like men. They wore the male ties and the masculine looking suits. Now the approach is to respect and understand all differences. People are coming into the workplace and they're saying, "Yes, I want to work with you toward your goal. I'm excited about it, but I want you to respect and understand the differences I bring to the workplace." So it's a totally different arena, and the effective manager will work to understand those differences.

I will give you a couple of examples. If you were a manager and had an Asian male working for you and were considering him for a promotion, if he were a traditional Asian male, typically he will not want to tout his own abilities. He will not want to talk to you about his excellent traits. He will talk about the fact that his team did this, and his division did this. You need to be an astute manager to be able to read between the lines and figure out what *he* personally contributed to the team and to the division. (This is where you need to be careful about stereotyping. You need to understand, pay attention, and observe so that you don't make a mistake.)

If you had an Indian woman, for example, who worked in your office and she drew a design of a widget (assuming you made widgets) and you held up that design in the office and said, "Isn't it wonderful? Look what she did!" Typically, if she were raised in the traditional Indian culture, this would be a poor way to deal with the situation, because she would be embarrassed by the attention. She might not come back to work the next day. She might even quit. In the Indian culture, it's not appropriate to have attention brought to yourself in that manner. So a manager would need to know that. A better way of dealing with that particular scenario would be to write up a nice letter to go in her file, so that when promotion time came around, that would be taken into consideration.

Diversity is a very complex thing where a great deal of knowledge is needed. And diversity, of course, applies to thinking globally as well.

During my presidential year in the National Speakers Association, I was extremely proud of the fact that a vision of mine—one that I had had as long as I can remember—came to pass. We formed the International Federation for Professional Speakers during my presidential year of National Speakers Association. I have long felt that the world's a very small place and the world can learn from professional speakers around the globe. So that's another part of diversity.

Wright

It's far reaching—a lot farther reaching than you suspect on the surface.

Most of the successful leaders I've interviewed tell me that they could not have made it without the help of others. Who in your life has been a mentor to you and helped you to become a successful leader?

Ball

That's an excellent question, and there are many, many people. But the first one who comes to mind is my dad. He was an encourager from as far back as I can remember. I started dance lessons at age two. In Dad's mind (and he said this to everyone he met), I was the most fantastic dancer that had ever existed on the earth. He constantly promoted my abilities. If there was something I couldn't do, he never let me believe that I was incapable of doing it or that it wasn't within my grasp—if I wanted it badly enough. He has helped me in every way throughout my life to reach my full potential.

Another person who comes to mind is my husband, Dr. Kenneth Ball, of more years than I care to mention here. Because of his background, he has been tremendously helpful in my career as well as in my life. He is a psychologist and was also president of a successful international company for sixteen years.

So of course, those two skills—practical management as well as theoretical—were very helpful to me in my Presidential year of National Speakers Association—in my work, and in my life.

I had a challenging year as President of National Speakers Association. I inherited a Board that was divided and filled with outspoken personalities. The Executive Vice President resigned the day before our first out-of-country conference held in Bermuda. And as a leader, I had to learn some very important skills. I had to find somebody to take the place of the Executive Vice President very quickly, and I did. I also learned that I had to communicate to many different kinds of groups. (Once again there's that word—communicate.) It was important for me to bring the past presidents in and have meetings with them, so that they would understand the dynamics of what was happening. Of course, we met with the Board a number of times and with the NSA staff, so they didn't feel left adrift. There were many things that happened, and it turns out that the National Speakers Association is going in an excellent direction these days.

The last person who comes to mind who acted as a mentor to me was the founder of the National Speakers Association, Cavett Robert. He is no longer living; he passed away September 15, 1997. He made you believe that anyone who had done anything at all could be phenomenally successful. I was excited by his vision of what the National Speakers Association and the speaking profession could become. I was excited about how he connected with speakers in the organization and got other people excited. That's my definition of a leader. He had a vision. He had a goal. He was able to get people to follow that vision and goal. He talked about having a bigger pie. Rather than everybody getting a piece of the pie, we just needed to make a bigger pie.

I was also flattered by him because (this is an amusing sideline) he used to call me "Wonder Woman." I had a passing resemblance to the woman who played Wonder Woman years ago—Linda Carter. Every time he saw me, he said, "Here comes Wonder Woman!"

Wright

He was a fine man. He encouraged me years ago, and I'll never forget him for doing that. We feel that leaders seem to believe in themselves. They seem to draw from some inner strength that others seem to either lack or not use properly. You have written extensively about inner strength. Will you tell our readers how to develop and use inner strength?

Ball

I believe it is something that develops over a long time. It has to do with self-esteem. My definition of self-esteem is simply liking yourself, accepting yourself for whom and what you are at that moment in time. Self-esteem comes about not only through positive experiences, but also in being able to handle failure, learning from failure, and being strengthened by them. It also has to do with a strong development of understanding ourselves and realistically judging ourselves, whether experiencing success or failure. It is being honest with ourselves about our performance.

When I have an excellent program, it's not necessarily the audience that tells me I was excellent, although it is frequently. When I have a program that I don't think is up to my usual standards, it's not necessarily the audience that tells me that either. I know within myself when I'm doing the best I can to the best of my ability and when I'm not. That's really what it's about. It's about accepting that failure, or challenge to be better, and moving forward.

It is really about choice. We make choices every day, all day long. We choose to find life a series of problems or exciting challenges. We choose to find people interesting or boring. We choose to be the best-informed, most attractive people we can be, or we choose to give up and blame others.

There is a fascinating premise I talk about sometimes in my programs. It is that the mind—our mind—doesn't really know the difference between truth and fiction. It believes anything we tell it. So if we put a negative thought in there, for example, "You're going to forget everything about this speech. You're not going to remember it. You'll draw a blank." The mind immediately says, "Oh, okay. That's what you want me to do," and it follows the dictate and forgets and draws a blank. So if you constantly feed your mind positive thoughts, like "Yes, I didn't do that as well as I could, but watch this next time!" you will continually move forward. It's a wonderful way to build that inner strength.

Wright

You know our book, *Leadership Defined*, is designed to help people to consider and become better leaders in their work, civic organizations, families, churches, and other endeavors simply because leaders like you took the time to bottom-line some of the qualities of leadership. Will you give us some of the characteristics that make leaders great—those things that they seem to have in common?

Ball

There are so many and it's fascinating to read all the books on leadership. Of course, yours is going to be at the top of the list.

Wright

We certainly hope so.

Ball

The first one that I think comes to mind is empathy. Empathy is the ability to connect with people, to read people well and understand people, to have excellent communication skills, and the ability to communicate concerns, and to communicate your vision and your goal.

Being able to walk the talk is certainly a significant factor. In other words, being an excellent role model yourself, not just talking about it, but also doing the things that you talk about.

Persistence is an important characteristic. Effective leaders I've known are extremely focused. They are persistent. They are goal oriented. They all have a vision. Many are future oriented. They don't simply observe the now, but they analyze trends and they look to see what that might mean for a future day. They have a great thirst for knowledge. They read everything they can get their hands on.

Effective leaders are risk-takers. They are not afraid of risks. They will examine what might be the outcome and the consequences of that risk and see how they can reduce the difficulty of taking that risk, but they are risk-takers.

Most leaders I know have a consistently positive attitude. That doesn't mean they never get down, but they are constantly thinking positively. They have a strong sense of self, confidence, and self-worth.

And finally, most effective leaders I know are assertive. That's a word that's gotten a bad rap over the years because a lot of people think assertiveness means aggressiveness. It doesn't. It simply means standing up for what you think is right.

Wright

My last question goes to your main focus in the speaking and training business. Knowing that communication is so important to be successful, happy, and have a fulfilled life, would you share with our readers what they can do to be better communicators of their ideas, dreams, and goals so that other people will want to help them succeed?

Ball

I think first and foremost they need to focus on becoming excellent listeners, using active listening, paying attention to other people, watching their non-verbal behavior, repeating what others say, giving them your undying attention, so they feel a sense of self-worth.

You need to learn to be a good observer. Concentrate on getting your cues from others through their body language, their silence, their tone of voice, their speed of speech, etc.

You need to become a straight talker. Take the shortest route to get the message across. Eliminate what I call "waffle words." These are words like "you know," and "whatever." You hear that a lot today. And phrases like, "it's only my opinion," and, "I don't know much about this, but . . . " All of those words and phrases rob your speech of power. You need to be brief with your speech. You need to learn to use silence.

And finally, you need to use what I call the "speech of positive intent." This means that, if you expect a successful outcome, you'll unconsciously choose straight-talking phrases. You'll choose those correct phrases because you expect to succeed. For example, instead of, "I'm only the secretary," you might say, "I'm the administrative assistant and I handle such and such." Instead of using the phrase, "I'll have to check on that for you," substitute the phrase, "I'll be happy to check on that." I'm sure you can hear the difference. It's a positive phraseology.

Being a successful communicator really boils down to continual learning. Never stop learning. Never stop trying new things. Never be discouraged when something doesn't work.

Wright

Well, what an exciting conversation. I learned a lot today, Patricia.

Ball

Thank you for the nice comments.

Wright

I could listen to you all day long. My business would be much better I'm sure.

Today we have been talking with Patricia Ball, CSP, CPAE. She is the President of Corporate Communications. She has helped thousands of executives, salespeople, and others achieve greater success in their personal and professional lives through the dramatic impact of her workshops and lectures. As we have found out today, she knows what she is talking about.

Thank you so much, Patricia, for being with us today on *Rising to the Top: A Guide to Success.*

Ball

It's been my pleasure.

About The Author

PATRICIA BALL, CSP, CPAE, is president of Corporate Communications. She served as a past national president of the National Speakers Association and a past International President of the International Federation for Professional Speakers. Patricia is a Certified Speaking Professional, communications specialist, keynoter, diversity trainer, author, and presentation skills coach. A graduate of Washington University, she has been on the lecture platform since 1972, speaking nationally and internationally. Patricia has helped thousands of executives, salespeople, and others achieve greater success in their personal and professional lives through the dramatic impact of her workshops and lectures.

In 1994, she was inducted into the CPAE (Council of Peers Award for Excellence) Speaker Hall of Fame—the "Oscar" of the speaking profession. As of this interview, less than 120 people worldwide had received this honor, and (in NSA's twenty-six-year history) only twenty-five women had been so recognized with both CSP and CPAE. Patricia has received intensive training in diversity and gender issues from the Copeland Griggs Institute in California.

Her superb talent for customizing programs to meet organizational needs has become her recognized trademark and has earned her the title of "The Speaker with the Dramatic Impact!" Patricia has a best-selling audio album called *Honing Your Presentation Skills,* and is the author of the book, *Straight Talk Is More Than Words,* which deals with how to be more persuasive and convincing.

Patricia Ball, CSP, CPAE
14312 Quiet Meadow Ct. E.
Chesterfield, Missouri 63017
Phone: 314.514.2455
E-mail: PatABall@aol.com

Chapter 14

LA MAR T. GUNN

THE INTERVIEW

David Wright (Wright)

Today we are talking with La Mar T. Gunn. He is a native of Los Angeles, California, and a graduate of the University of Delaware. Upon graduation he made Wilmington, Delaware, his home and has since committed himself to building his community. In his capacity as financial advisor and chief investment strategist with Gunn Financial, his business mission is to be an indispensable wealth management resource for his clients. He designs sophisticated strategies to help high net-worth clients create and protect wealth. Not only does La Mar provide sound guidance for his clients, but he also provides sage leadership to the community at large by promoting a "live to win" philosophy through educational and motivational lectures. La Mar views life as a journey of lessons and uses what he has learned along the way to help others. He also values honesty and respect, and displays those qualities to his family, friends, clients, community, and everyone he encounters.

La Mar, welcome to *Rising to the Top: A Guide to Success.*

La Mar T. Gunn (Gunn)
Thank you, David; it's my pleasure!

Wright
What is the biggest secret between the rich and the poor?

Gunn
That is an interesting question, but it escapes most of us. Through all my years of research, I've found that the one difference between the rich and the poor is simple: it's attitude!

Wright
You mean as in positive against negative?

Gunn
Positive against negative is one point, but there's another piece: attitude as opposed to "fear." Fear is really simple, but most people don't seem to get it. F.E.A.R. is nothing more than False Evidence (or emotions) Appearing Real. Attitude has a negative impact on so many aspects of our lives, and in many cases, it keeps people from achieving or reaching the top. Aspects of a negative attitude include self-doubt, timidity, worry, negative people, excuses, self-pity, and procrastination. These attitudes cause stumbling blocks that stand in the way of people really achieving the things that they want or, even more importantly, living the life they want.

Wright
How do you think people can improve their vision for the future?

Gunn
I always encourage folks to go out and purchase more books and add them to their libraries. I've heard it said that, "Rich people have large libraries, while poor people have large televisions!" At my conferences, I always ask my attendees, "Which one do you have?" I always encourage them to have at least the one book I consider to be the best book ever written on "vision:" the Bible.

Proverbs 29:18 states, "Where there is no vision, the people perish." If you want to learn how to achieve success in life or learn about making money or about creating wealth, from real estate to the stock market, or even how to run your own business and to improve your vision, the Bible is a fantastic place to start!

Wright

Why do you believe people should avoid the concept of "paying themselves first"?

Gunn

I hear that concept all the time, and that's another stumbling block that probably keeps people from reaching that ultimate level of success. They've got it all backward! I totally disagree with the pundits out there who promote the concept of "paying yourself first" as a way of creating financial success. From a normal viewpoint, "pay yourself first" makes perfect sense. I am all for people taking care of themselves; but, from a Biblical perspective, that is out of order. In my own life, I found that by paying myself *second,* I've received unlimited blessings. And what do I mean by that? It's pretty simple: pay unto God's kingdom first, meaning give your tithe. When you do that, blessings just seem to overflow.

My advice is to pay yourself first *after* giving your tithe. I always tell people that when it comes to money and paying bills and so forth, of course you have to pay your utility bills, etc. Remember there's one important thing: if you look at the first letter of the word "Utility," it's a "U"! I want you to pay yourself, but just keep it in perspective and go with the proper system of things, which is paying yourself second. I've noticed that, since I started tithing and paying into other people's visions by sowing seeds to help them, the blessings that come back to me have been unbelievable.

Wright

What can we learn from running our lives and finances like a business?

Gunn

As a stockbroker, I analyze companies. The best companies usually run a tight ship on a day-to-day basis. Of course you have the company motto and so forth, and there's usually a system or outline of things that need to be accomplished each day. There are goals, and most companies are judged by a quarterly report or an earnings report that gives them something to shoot for. But in our personal lives, we usually don't have anything to guide us along the way. There aren't any lamps lit along the road that say, "Hey, follow this path!" When we can follow and construct our lives like a business meeting, *we have a game plan!*

I put together a game plan of how a person's life is going to run on a day-to-day basis, I make some long- and short-term goals and set things in priority. If it's finances, I encourage that person to set a goal that is both desirable and attainable. When you run your life like a business, you become organized. You will have structure instead of living life like a carnival bumper car ride, going in whatever direction that life or day-to-day challenges knock you. You'll have a system in place to help you stay focused.

I'm sure you've heard this time and time again, but it makes perfect sense: "If you fail to plan, you plan to fail!" I want people to remember that, and to focus on it. This is nothing new—speakers have used it time and time again; but it all really comes out of the scriptures, which is a great place to start!

Wright

You talk a lot about the importance of strategic partnerships. What do you mean by that?

Gunn

It is my firm belief that if we look at strategic partnerships, we see a team. I'm big on acronyms, so let's break it down: TEAM = "Together Everyone Achieves More."

I'm a big fan of teams and the power of more than one. Here's a quick example: One Clydesdale horse can pull about five tons. Do you have any idea what two can do?

Wright

I'd say that you have synergism coming in, so probably more than twice that.

Gunn

How about *five times* as much? Just by combining forces, two Clydesdales can pull twenty-five tons! That's just an example as to what we can do if we pull together. A lot of people get stuck in the mentality of saying, "Hey, I want to do this all by myself" and they program themselves for mediocrity. You have to look at it from the standpoint that it *does* take teamwork to make the dream work! That hopefully gives you a good idea as to what I mean when I talk about strategic partners.

Here's another example. Say you have a business and you are an attorney; in my case I'm a stockbroker. There's a huge opportunity for us to help each other. I can refer clients to you who need estate planning and trust work, etc., and you can refer a lot of business to me as well. Instead of the whole competitive "dog-eat-dog" mentality, we develop more of a "dog-feed-dog" synergistic relationship. When you form a strategic partnership, you put yourself in that Olympic class type of athlete as far as your performance.

Wright

How can people create multiple streams of income and find an easier way into the stock market?

Gunn

This goes back to teamwork. I've recently been encouraging people to go out and create small pockets of investment clubs. The stock market has been a mystery to many people for several years. One way to demystify things is to pull together as a team or a unit and to form an investment club. Familiarize yourself with the basic principles as far as the stock market. If you keep it simple you'll find that it's not as difficult or as crazy as some people make it out to be. When it becomes over-aggressive and crazy is when you suffer losses.

There are a couple of basic things to remember when going into the stock market. Unfortunately we don't have time to get into all of them today, but these items are important. The stock market is a risk-controlled situation. You don't have to follow that system of buying and holding. You hear all these stories about people losing all their money. Take the Enron situation, where all those folks invested their life savings into the market and followed the advice of the pundits who told them, "Hold on, hold on, it will come back." But that was completely wrong and just plain old *bad* advice. Had they just followed one of the basic rules of investing, they would have been alright. Rule number one is: "Don't lose money!" And Rule number two is: "Don't forget Rule number one!"

Let me explain the strategy to you. In the stock market, you have the ability to do something called "limit losses." You do that with something called a Stop Order, and here's what it does: Let's say I want to buy McDonald's shares and the rate is fifty dollars per share. In the event that my choice was wrong and I begin to lose money, I want out of this position at 10 to 15 percent. I put in a Stop Order, and it activates. It tells my broker that we want to initiate a sale at forty-five dollars a share—at 10 percent to the downside we want out. It happens automatically, and it takes the emotion out of investing. It allows people who don't have a lot of knowledge to grow into the stock market gradually instead of getting wiped out within the first few years or even months.

Now here's the biggest secret to achieving wealth in the stock market: limit your losses. To take it even further, as far as getting your toe into the water, I always tell people to start out with the investment club, and then go with something along the overall stock market type of fund. I suggest something along the lines of an S&P 500 Fund until you can get a feel for things. You can always take it to the next level after that.

Wright

One of the things I've been reading on the Internet and news wires is about foreclosures all over the country. How do you think we can help each other through what seems like a national disaster with all these foreclosures taking place in America?

Gunn

I'll tell you, David, it seems like our government is always a little too late to the party. With the number of sub-prime deals taking place over the past few years, and folks using their houses like ATM machines when it comes to refinancing and home equity, people have gotten into a ton of trouble.

I truly believe that within the next few years, we are going to have a complete elimination of the middle class. This means people are either going to be rich or poor. Foreclosures continue to climb. Estimates are that one in every four houses purchased and financed over the next few years will also go into foreclosure. Based on the fact of a failing economy (and that the United States really doesn't have any loyalty anymore when it comes to corporations and big business), it's all about making money and delivering value to the shareholders.

How do we help each other in this foreclosure situation? Some of us, especially some of us in the Baby Boom Generation are in a position to help. These are the ones who are starting to retire; they have excess cash and they're looking to do things with it other than investing in the standard 2 or 3 percent CD. In keeping with the spirit of wanting to help people, you can actually help yourself and your family and push your financial status into an entirely different stratosphere just by helping somebody else in need.

Here's how that works: For the folks who have cashed in on the sideline and with the increasing foreclosure rates, there are going to be huge opportunities in real estate. Yes, foreclosures are rising, but what does that mean? It's an opportunity for folks who want to become investors to step in and actually do some good at the same time.

Say for instance there's a family of three led by a single mother. Maybe she's lost her job or maybe she's gone through a divorce recently. Maybe she has gotten behind on her bills and is in a position where she might lose her property. As an angel type of investor, you can step in and say, "You know what, Mrs. Jackson? You have something to work with here. Your mortgage is $100,000 but your property is appraised at $200,000."

Because Mrs. Jackson has been late on a couple of payments she can't even refinance the estate. The banks see the equity in the property and they move to foreclose so they can protect their interests. You as the investor can say, "Hey, here's what we'll do: Allow me to come in, make up your payments, get the mortgage caught up, and let's put the house on the market for sale. I'll do that for you to get you out of the situation of losing everything, and in good faith, we split the profits." In this case it's a matter of personal choice or preference as to the percentages, whether you go with 50/50, or 60/40, it's 100 percent up to you. But whatever the percentage comes to, the important thing is that you save people from having a foreclosure on their credit record. It takes years for a foreclosure to be removed from a credit report—it's almost like a type of credit suicide. It winds up costing you thousands of dollars, maybe more going forward. If you wind up with bad credit, everything into the future is going to cost you more money because of the higher interest rates that you'll attract.

Hopefully that answers the question. I advise people to look to help somebody. If you use your financial position to help someone avoid foreclosure, you're going to set yourself up for many years going forward. And as the Bible says, "The wise man prepares for his children's children." With real estate and the increase in foreclosures taking place, there is a tremendous opportunity to come into a situation, to help those who are less fortunate and to leave a really tremendous legacy through all of the profits you will be able to make for your children.

I've seen lives ruined over just a few instances of bad judgment in the way people have financed their properties. The American Dream is almost the American Nightmare. I could go on about this topic all day, but I'm sure you have other questions.

Wright

You believe that people will be either rich or poor in the coming years. What do you see as some of our opportunities? Are there any other ways we can find opportunities?

Gunn

There are many opportunities out there! I go out and speak to groups in churches all around the country and to community groups and so forth, just trying to educate people about these types of opportunities. Of course there's the stock market, if you can get in there. Maybe you don't have the wherewithal to start or run your own business, but if you're making money, you can buy in on a great business or two. How many people use the drive-through of a fast food restaurant (i.e., McDonald's or Taco Bell)? And that's just it. People should start thinking, "Hey, since the stock market is so simple, I could just buy the things I use every day." We've talked about that opportunity.

With a little over three hundred million people in the United States and the economy sputtering along, there's another place where I would like people to focus their attention: overseas. Whether we like it or not, all of our jobs are going overseas. Right now, for every American engineer, you can have four Chinese engineers. They are set to graduate over 700,000 engineers in the next eighteen months. How can we compete with that? We can't! "Made in America" used to mean something, but not anymore. The Chinese are doing the jobs we once had for pennies on the dollar. It used to be mainly manufacturing jobs such as the auto industry. In fact, in Detroit, where a lot of auto manufacturing is based, foreclosures are among the highest in the country. But it's just not happening in those manufacturing towns anymore. As we start to lose jobs in the science field, banking, or legal industry, we're heading for something that looks to be cataclysmic.

Let's go back to opportunities. I've always heard it said, "If you can't beat 'em, join 'em," and I say that loosely. What I want folks to look at is how you can make money from the growth and the boom going on over in Asia and places like India. There are hidden gems called Africa and Brazil with tons of opportunities there. How do you access them? Look at what's going on in China for example. What do the Chinese need most? Resources! Some of my clients have made pretty good money over the past few years by helping the Chinese meet their need for natural resources and products and so forth. Since they didn't (and don't) have enough, they've had to import things. The United States is very heavy in shipping goods to China.

One major export now is concrete. Think about it. Skyscrapers are going up left and right, and expanding all the way out to the countryside. China is experiencing industrialization as never before. All the building they're doing makes New York look like a small town in Montana. Where are they getting all the concrete and materials with which to build? From us! They have a need for natural resources, so there's an opportunity for you as a businessperson.

Look into the stock market and buy companies that sell things to the Chinese. If you've started a business, make sure you have a product line that can focus on a system or a country where they have billions of people ready to buy American products.

Don't let a negative attitude convince you to say, "Okay, I've just lost my job. It's been outsourced to India or China, and now I'm just going to wither away." Instead, take the right attitude and figure out a way to make lemonade out of the lemons you've been dealt.

In those buildings that are going up left and right, what else do the Chinese need? We found a huge demand for copper! Some people may say, "Why copper?" Guess what all those buildings have running all through them? No, not just plumbing—it's wires! Copper is in every wire, and they need tons and tons of it to go in each and every building.

Another resource is yellow cake (and no I don't mean what Mom makes for Sunday dinner). This is another scientific term for a substance called uranium oxide. It's a new source of energy. We know about oil and gas, but the smart money is going toward uranium oxide. The Chinese have this well figured out, and nuclear reactors are going up everywhere in those countries. There's only one problem: they need uranium to power those facilities. They don't have it, which means they have to go out and buy it. Places that have it, like the United States and Australia, are in a great position to go out and deliver unbelievable wealth to people who can figure this out and get in on this huge opportunity. Whether you're rich or poor, if you can take advantage of opportunities like these, it places you "in the know."

I can't even begin to tell you how important it is to have some sort of exposure to nuclear power in the upcoming years. Oil made folks filthy rich, so why aren't we taking advantage when new energy sources surface?

I don't want people to suffer from this disease I often call "excusitis." Folks have to look for and research these types of opportunities, and start making some money. I could go on and on and on with opportunities all day if you like, but I'm sure there's another question.

Wright

Finally, let me ask you this: is there anything else that the wealthy do that we can begin to apply to our day-to-day lives?

Gunn

Sure, I've found that most of them have some strong sense of or belief in God. The other thing is that they are master planners. I touched on that earlier. Many of us don't have any sort of written plan. People have an idea about "what" and "where" they want to be in the future, but when they do things like that I tell them those aren't goals and vague ideas are not plans. If your goals and your plans are not written, *they are nothing more than dreams.* If you're really serious, and you want to live like wealthy people do, you have to first start emulating them. Watch how they act. Go out and do the same, and then lead others by your example.

The one thing I can share that wealthy people do is really simple—they have a game plan! You may be living paycheck to paycheck today, but you don't have to live that way tomorrow. If you have a plan and you believe in it, you work it, you stick to it. In fact, if there's a turn or a curve, so be it. Just take it and keep moving!

I used to coach Little League football. Ten years out of twelve when I coached, we won the little league championship. I couldn't believe it, but I realized the other kids in their teams and their coaches never had a plan. So, even with something as simple as Little League sports, I was able to have more success. My players were able to experience victory more often simply because we went into each game with a plan. Even at the professional level, do we actually think that Phil Jackson, Bill Parcells, Bill Belichick, or any of these guys go into a game without a plan? Of course not! You can even see these guys with huge scripts now on the sidelines. But what do we do in life? We don't have anything written down—we don't have a plan.

Here is one strategy that you can apply to your everyday life: Take a regular sheet of paper and at the top of it write "Number One". Let this be your goal. So write your goal at the top of the piece of paper. Just keep this simple; we're going to call this strategy "One, Two, Three."

One is the goal. Next, you're going to come up with two reasons why you want to achieve that goal. Write them down, and believe in them.

Next, you're going to list three ways to achieve it. So you have the goal, you have why you want to achieve the goal and you have some plans on how you're going to achieve the goal!

The final piece is to add a deadline. If you simply put plans together without a time limit, you're never going to accomplish them. You have to set a deadline for yourself in order to be accountable for finishing what you started.

Another thing that I can add for families is to make these plans public. It just might not be just Mom and Dad's goals—you can get the kids involved. Place little notes around the house where your children can see them so they can participate, and it becomes a family mission to achieve the goals that are set. I call this process "visioneering." I'm visioneering the way to success and following some of the habits of the wealthy.

We must start reading more. Our ancestors would have killed to read. Today you have to practically kill most people to get them to read. We have to give back what has made America so strong and successful, and that's discipline, savings and a focus on education.

Video games, not parents, are teaching our children and it doesn't look good for our future! We need to pump the brakes, get back into the driver's seat of our lives and get this country back on track.

About the Author

LA MAR T. GUNN, a native of Los Angeles, California, is a graduate of the University of Delaware. Upon graduation, La Mar made Wilmington, Delaware, his home, and has since committed himself to building his community. In his capacity as a Financial Advisor and Chief Investment Strategist with Gunn Financial, La Mar's business mission is to be an indispensable wealth management resource for his clients. He designs sophisticated strategies to help high net worth clients create and protect wealth. Not only does La Mar provide sound guidance for his clients, he also provides sage leadership to the community at large by promoting a "live to win" philosophy through educational and motivational lectures. Viewing life as a journey of lessons, La Mar uses what he has learned along the way to help others. He also values honesty and respect, and displays those qualities to his family, friends, clients, community, and everyone he encounters.

La Mar T. Gunn
Phone: 302.832.9277
E-mail: lgunn@lamargunn.com
www.lamargunn.com